NEW ENGLAND TURKEY HUNTING
Strategies for Success

The Complete Guide to Turkey Hunting in New England

By Bob Humphrey

Edited by
James Ehlers

NEW ENGLAND TURKEY HUNTING
Strategies for Success

Published by

Sport-Ventures
727 Poland Range Road
Pownal, Maine 04069
Telephone: (207) 688-4966
www.bobhumphrey.com

Photography: Bob Humphrey
Book Design: Bob Humphrey and Elk Publishing, Inc.
Cover Design: Elk Publishing, Inc.

Library of Congress Control Number:
2003090454
ISBN 0-9724797-0-8

Printed in the United States of America

dedication

To the future generations of turkey hunters

acknowledgments

There are so many individuals and groups that helped this project come to fruition, and in trying to name them I run the risk of leaving some out. Just the same, I owe special gratitude to the following: First and foremost to my wife, Jane, for putting up with my absences every spring, standing by me during the lean times and encouraging me to pursue my dream; Richard G. Bernier, who kept me on track in pursuing this endeavor; Stu Bristol, one of my mentors as an outdoor writer; Jim Wescott, for his insight on fall hunting; Jim Casada, for sharing his advice and insight into the publishing world; and Mark Luthman, for sharing the zeal with me on all of those early turkey hunts.

I would also like to thank the following for their assistance in gathering statistics and historical information contained in several chapters: Brad Allen, Phil Bozenhard and Andy Weik, Maine Department of Inland Fisheries & Wildlife; Ted Walski, New Hampshire Fish & Game Department; Doug Blodgett and John Hall, Vermont Department of Fish & Wildlife; Jim Cardoza and Bill Davis, MassWildlife; Mike Gregonis and Howard Kilpatrick, Connecticut Department of Environmental Protection; and Brain Tefft, Rhode Island Department of Environmental Management.

Special thanks also to the many volunteers from the various state chapters of the National Wild Turkey Federation for all their efforts, and to New England's dairy farmers for giving the turkeys a place to live, and us sportsmen a place to hunt.

contents

Foreword 7
Introduction 13

PART 1. NATURAL HISTORY & HISTORY
1. The Wild Turkey 17
2. Four Seasons 31
3. Return of the Thanksgiving Bird 45
4. Ongoing Management Efforts 59

PART 2. HUNTING EQUIPMENT & TECHNIQUES
5. Clothing 73
6. Guns & Ammo 85
7. Gearing Up for Gobblers 101
8. Scout Now, Score Later 111
9. Calls & Calling 123
10. The Setup 151
11. Advanced Tactics 163
12. Bowhunting 175
13. Fall Hunting 187

PART 3. WHERE TO GO—STATE BY STATE
14. Northern New England 201
15. Southern New England 217

PART 4. WRAP-UP
16. Turkey Hunting Etiquette & Safety 231
17. Scoring Your Turkey 241
18. Preserving Your Trophy 251

Appendices
1. Sources of Information 263
2. Turkey Hunter's Checklist 269

Glossary 271

foreword

Make no doubt about it, for turkey hunters the "good old days" are the present. Thanks to one of the greatest wildlife comeback sagas in the history of conservation, populations of the American wild turkey are at an all-time high in almost all of the 49 states (plus several Canadian provinces) where various subspecies of the bird are found.

Virtually all of this has come about in the last half century. At the turn of the 20th century, turkey numbers were terribly low, and American's big-game bird had been extirpated in many areas. Hunters and conservationists recognized the problem, but all their early efforts at restoration were abysmal failures. These included stocking pen-raised birds, attempts to cross wild turkeys with domestic ones, hatching eggs from wild turkeys and raising the poults, and the like. None worked, for as we now know turkeys reared in captivity imprint on humans and lose the wariness essential to their survival in the wild. Adding to the problem was a widespread belief that wild turkeys could only survive in large areas of mature timber (5,000 acres was generally believed to be a minimal requirement).

All of this changed with the advent of trap and transfer methods of stocking turkeys. Using rocket nets to trap wild turkeys, usually brought to the net by baiting a suitable site for a number of days, the birds could be moved to another place and proved quite capable of establishing themselves in a new home. One state wildlife agency after another adopted this method, and from the early 1970s on they received appreciable and important support from the National Wild Turkey Federation. The result, as these words are being written early in 2003, is a success story in which all concerned can take pride. It has also meant vastly expanded opportunities for hunters.

That's where this book enters the equation. When turkeys were scarce, the literature of the sport was sparse indeed. In 1950, at the dawn of the trap and transfer era, only four or five books on turkey hunting had been written. Today, my personal turkey hunting library numbers upwards of 400 volumes, and at least half of them are devoted exclusively to understanding and hunting this wonderful sporting quarry. One of these books deals with basically the same geographic area covered in the present work. This is Stewart Bristol's *Hunting Wild Turkeys in New England* (1986). A second book, Chuck Collinge's *Nutmeg Turkeys: A Guide to the Wild Turkey in Connecticut* (1992), is also relevant, albeit with a narrower geographic scope.

Both books are interesting and, for the time at which they were written, quite useful. However, there have been vast changes in the turkey hunting situation in New England since their publication. For starters, equipment, from an amazing array of calls to special purpose guns and all sorts of accessories, has advanced light years in the course of less than a generation. Additionally, there are far more turkeys (and turkey hunters) in the region than was the case a decade or a decade and a half ago. We have a better understanding of how to hunt, regulations and seasons have altered and many other changes have transpired. All of this adds up to the fact that this book is timely and much needed.

The author is eminently qualified for his task. He belongs to the school of woodsmen my grandfather used to describe as "hard hunters." That is to say, individuals who take their sport seriously, go about it in a fashion where their dedication is matched only by their sporting ethics, and realize that in the school of the outdoors graduation day never arrives. Folks who study in this school, such as Bob Humphrey, invariably make first-rate hunters. They are observant, ever eager to obtain new knowledge, students of their prey, and equipped with a mindset that absorbs new knowledge like a sponge.

Perhaps sharing some personal experiences with the author might provide an even better understanding of why I'm delighted to see this book come to fruition. We joined veteran hunter and well-known turkey personality Brad Harris, of Lohman Calls, for a Midwest hunt a few years back. I was working on a book on Harris and another noted caller and callmaker, Mark Drury (the book was published in 2000 under the title *Innovative Turkey Hunting*). To be perfectly honest, I was a bit concerned when Brad told me another sporting scribe would be joining us, because I knew I needed to do a great deal of photo work, not to mention hours of interview, in order to get the material I needed for the book.

My reservations could not have been more misplaced. Bob proved to be a congenial camp companion, a skilled and patient hunter and a real help to me when it came to getting some of my photographic work done. The trip also provided a delightful moment that offered some laughs even as it attested to Bob's standing as a hunter. I had already

One of the best parts about turkey hunting is the people you get to share time afield with. I was privileged to share a turkey hunt several years ago with Jim Casada.

taken my limit of two birds, and Bob had a fine longbeard to his credit as well. In company with Brad, we crossed a rickety and picturesque old swinging bridge to a promising area, and eventually I spotted a turkey in the distance.

Eventually, thanks to Brad's seductive calling and some snake-like sneaking by Bob as he got into position, they managed to get the bird in for a shot. Unfortunately, it was at an extremely awkward angle. Bob crippled the tom, and that's when the fun began. The race was on, and after he had emptied his gun while pursuing the tom, it all came down to foot speed. Bob shed calls, cap, vest and all sorts of paraphernalia in the course of a world-class 440-yard run, but when we caught up with him he had his prize in hand. A lesser man, or one with less determination, might well have lost that grand bird. We all had a good laugh, exchanged congratulatory high fives, and all the while I thought to myself—this fellow will do just fine.

Since that escapade some five years ago, we've kept in touch and I've watched Bob, who utilizes his background training as a wildlife biologist to good advantage, rise in stature as a writer. His byline increasingly appears in national publications, and as the pages that follow reveal, he's a man who has, as the lingo goes, "been there and done that." Here he writes on a subject and an area he knows intimately, and the result is a book everyone who hunts this part of the country should have on their shelves. Furthermore, there's plenty of sound stuff here for turkey hunters no matter where they hang their hat. The book makes a fine addition to the growing list of important books on turkey hunting, and it is a notable first book from a promising writer.

Jim Casada
1250 Yorkdale Drive
Rock Hill, SC 29730-7638
E-mail: jimcasada@comporium.net

introduction

As I stepped out of my truck into the dim gray light of dawn, I heard a chorus of barred owls, challenging one another with their eerie hoots. They were so close it made the hair stand up on the back of my neck. The robins, thrushes and warblers were just beginning to chime in when, somewhere down in distance, I heard a gobble—my very first. It seemed almost prehistoric, as if the bird was calling as much from the depths of time as the valley below.

I raced down the hill, stopping to catch my breath, and listened again—more gobbles. Soon it seemed as though I was surrounded by gobbling turkeys. I'd hunted hard for days without hearing so much as a yelp, and now, with the opportunity I'd longed for so close at hand, panic began to set in. I didn't have a clue what to do.

I heard another gobble, still well below me, so I darted downhill another 50 yards and plopped down against a big oak, gasping as much from excitement as exertion. Then I heard another gobble, this time off to my right. "He's gonna get by me," I thought, and I raced off in that direction, but before I could sit, I heard another gobble from below and yet another below and to my left. The birds had me bouncing around the woods like a human pinball, trying to find the right place to set up, and in the process I managed to frighten them all off.

I cursed myself for squandering such a precious opportunity. At that time turkeys were few and far between, and close encounters were fewer still. I also admonished myself for lack of preparation, but good advice on how to hunt turkeys was even harder to come by than the turkeys themselves back then.

Things certainly have changed over the last 15 to 20 years with regard to turkey hunting in the six New England states. Twenty years ago only four of the six states even had turkey seasons. Turkey populations in those states were still relatively small and hunter participation, success rates and annual kills were low as well.

Growth in the sport and in turkey populations was at first slow. As turkeys gradually expanded their range and their numbers increased, so did interest in pursuing them. Over the last half-dozen years however, turkey populations and interest in turkey hunting have skyrocketed across the six-state region, and both the hunting fraternity and turkey numbers continue to grow each year. This book is in part an acknowledgment of that phenomenon.

Along with a nationwide growth of interest in the sport has come a plethora of information on turkey hunting. Each spring, outdoor magazines are filled with advice on how to hunt turkeys, and there are at least two national magazines devoted solely to the sport. In addition, you can find dozens of turkey hunting videos on the racks at your local sporting good store, and cable television channels abound with shows filled with turkey hunting action. This is all great information for novice and experienced turkey hunters alike. However, one thing noticeably missing from most of these resources is information specifically directed toward our region—New England.

While the turkey hunting craze has spread from coast to coast and border to border, New England has very quietly grown into one of the top turkey regions in the country. Over the last 15 years, hunter numbers have swollen, yet relatively little information has been disseminated on how and where to hunt local birds.

That is another reason for this book. While much of the general "how-to" advice in the national media can be applied to turkeys in New England, Yankee birds, like their pursuers, have there own idiosyncrasies. Furthermore, a big part in being successful involves knowing where to go.

For the past five years I have annually contacted turkey biologists from each of the six New England states, some of whom I have known personally and professionally for considerably longer, to seek their expertise on where the best odds for turkey hunting success lie. Over that same span, I have also visited and hunted in many of those same areas.

The information contained in this book is a culmination of my own experiences hunting throughout the region, and the advice and opinion of professionals from each state, many of whom work on a daily basis with the turkeys in their respective states.

There is one other reason I felt compelled to write this book. When I began hunting turkeys in New England, there was little information available. Much of what I learned came through trial and error, sometimes lots of error. It was a slow process, but in the long run, I feel better off for being a self-taught turkey hunter. However, I'd venture to guess most hunters would rather take the fast track, learning as much as they can about the sport before they go afield, so they don't squander those precious opportunities. Since my years as a teaching assistant in college, I have felt a calling to teach, and share my knowledge with those anxious and willing to learn. I have also gained a great deal of satisfaction in doing so. Thus, this effort was a labor of love.

Read on, learn and enjoy.

one

THE WILD TURKEY

one

If I close my eyes and let my mind wander a bit, I can conjure up memories of my first close encounter with a wild turkey. It came not during my first hunting season, but the year I started taking turkey hunting seriously. Birds were pretty scarce back then around most parts of New England, and you had to do a lot of looking before you actually found one. I'd spent two frustratingly silent days wandering the hill towns of the western Connecticut River valley with little to show for my efforts but sore feet. Providence came one afternoon in the form of a hot lead. I spent the rest of the day scouting, and found enough sign to give this new spot a try.

I arrived well in advance of daylight the next morning, drove up the long woods road, and pulled in under a grove of old hemlocks. With plenty of time to spare, I decided to sit back, listen to the radio and enjoy my coffee. Over the rhythmic notes of some long-forgotten rock 'n roll song I heard a clamor outside, so I shut off the radio and stepped out into the inky-black morning. That's when I heard them.

Several barred owls were exchanging their characteristic "who-cooks-for-you; who-cooks-for-you-all" calls back and forth across the big softwood grove. The cacophony soon prompted another, almost primordial sound from the valley below, a sound that set my heart to pounding: the gobble of the wild turkey. That gobble was followed by several more, and soon it sounded as though the whole valley was filled with turkeys. It looked like I would finally get my chance to challenge the king of game birds.

I hastily grabbed my vest and gun, and raced off down the hill into the darkness. Birds were gobbling from every direction, and I frantically searched for just the right ambush spot. I finally found a huge oak situated on a small bench. The trunk of this ancient tree was twice the width of my shoulders, and as I settled in among its buttressed roots, I considered that it must have been around during a time long-ago, when turkeys were much more numerous.

I popped in a diaphragm call and began a rather pathetic rendition of a lonely hen. I was a total neophyte, and things happened so quickly I really didn't know how to react. Somehow, I managed to botch several opportunities, and though I left the woods that morning without a bird, I had my first real lesson in turkey hunting. It was several more seasons before I finally took my first gobbler.

Having no mentors to teach me the finer points of turkey hunting, my longbeard lessons came mostly from trial and lots of error. It was a long, slow and often frustrating process. But I believe learning the hard way ultimately made me a better turkey hunter. However, the purpose of this book is to make *you* a better turkey hunter.

If you had the time, you could probably head into the woods "cold turkey" and, in two or three seasons, learn enough to be consistently successful on your own. But how many of us would be willing to devote that much time, even if we had it? Besides, it's much easier to learn from the mistakes of others than those of your own. And when it comes to making mistakes, I consider myself an expert. My only saving grace is that I have been able to learn from each and every one of those mistakes.

One of the most important lessons I've learned about hunting turkeys, as well as other game, is to be a student of the animal you pursue. Knowing techniques like how to use certain types of calls is useful, but if you don't why you're using them, or when they're most effective, their utility is limited. For example: What should you do if a gobbling tom comes racing uphill toward you, only to stop 75 yards away, and continues to gobble but comes no closer? What should you do if a bird that's been gobbling up a storm suddenly goes mum? Should you move closer, or should you stay put? These scenarios are quite common, and while experience may give you a hint to the answer, knowing what's going on inside the turkey's walnut-sized brain can also be a genuine asset.

So let's begin with a basic introduction to the wild turkey. The more you know about turkeys, the better turkey hunter you'll be. Then you can begin concentrating on the finer points. This knowledge will also make for a safer and more enjoyable hunt. Hearing a turkey gobble is thrilling, but understanding why he's gobbling will give you a much greater appreciation for what you're about to become a part of as you move in to challenge him.

BIOLOGICALLY SPEAKING

Taxonomically, the turkey is a member of the order *Galliformes.* This order includes a variety of chicken-like birds including pheasants, quail, turkeys and, yes, chickens. Gallinaceous birds are characterized by strong legs and feet, which are used to scratch for food; short, rounded wings designed for brief, rapid flight; and a short, stout beak for pecking.

Wild turkeys belong to a group of gallinaceous, or chicken-like, birds that feed on a variety of nuts, seeds, green vegetation and insects. Males are distguishable from females by their larger size, darker color and beards and spurs, which the females lack.

Five recognized subspecies of the wild turkey occur in North America. The Rio Grande turkey occupies a range that spans roughly from Kansas, south through Texas and into northeastern Mexico, with scattered populations in California and Oregon. The range of the Merriam's is scattered across the Northwest, Southwest and Mountain States. The Osceola, or Florida subspecies, is restricted to Florida, approximately from Orlando, south. The Gould's is more common in Mexico, with small populations ranging north into New Mexico. The Eastern is the largest and most widespread, occurring in all states east of the Mississippi River, and ranging west into eastern portions of the Plains States and Texas. Thus, in New England we're talking about the Eastern wild turkey.

VIVE LA DIFFERENCE

All races of wild turkeys are sexually dimorphic, meaning males and females have different physical characteristics. Adult males average 17 to 21 pounds, while smaller females average eight to 11 pounds. The

By their second spring, young males or "jakes" typically sport a beard that is three to five inches long.

contour, or body, feathers of males are black-tipped, giving the birds an overall blackish color. Those of the females are buff-tipped, making them appear more brownish. The naked, nearly featherless head of the female is bluish-gray in color, while that of the male is more red. During the breeding season, especially when he's puffed up strutting, the male's head becomes a brilliant red, white and blue. The front of his head is also adorned with a slender, fleshy appendage at the base of the bill. Called a "snood," it becomes elongated and dangles beside the head when the bird is excited.

Beards

A somewhat reliable way to distinguish hens from male birds, or "gobblers," is by the gobbler's beard. This appendage is actually modified feathers and dangles from the gobbler's breast. Beards grow roughly three to five inches a year. A one-year-old male sporting a beard of this length is called a "jake." The beard of a two-year-old male is typically eight to ten inches, and from this point on he is called a "tom." For the first three years, a gobbler's beard will be amber-tipped.

Though rare, hens occasionally sport beards. Though they are legal game, they are otherwise perfectly normal and can mate and raise a brood. Thus, hunters should refrain from taking them in the spring.

After that, it will appear entirely black. The beard continues to grow throughout the gobbler's life, though growth slows in later years. After a beard gets much past 12 inches, the ends begin to wear off. In northern regions, like New England, the beard tips may become encrusted with ice and break off. Some birds will experience "beard rot," a malady believed to be from a parasitic infection. Such beards are often shorter and the ends appear frayed and lighter in color. In these cases, beard length is not a reliable indicator of age.

About four percent of hens have beards, and gobblers may occasionally lack them altogether. Typically, a gobbler has one beard, though they may sport several. According to records from the National Wild Turkey Federation, the most beards ever recorded on a single bird is nine.

Spurs

Males sport spurs on their metatarsus, or lower leg, while females generally lack them. Spurs are sometimes a better indicator of age than are beards. A jake will typically have short, rounded spurs of one-half inch or less. The spurs of a two-year-old generally range from five-eighths to seven-eighths of an inch. At age three, a tom may have spurs of one inch or slightly longer. By age four, the spurs may be 1 1/4 to 1 1/2 inches. As the spurs grow longer, they become sharper and more hooked. Older turkeys, whose spurs are long and hooked enough to allow the bird to be hung from a tree limb, are called "limbhangers."

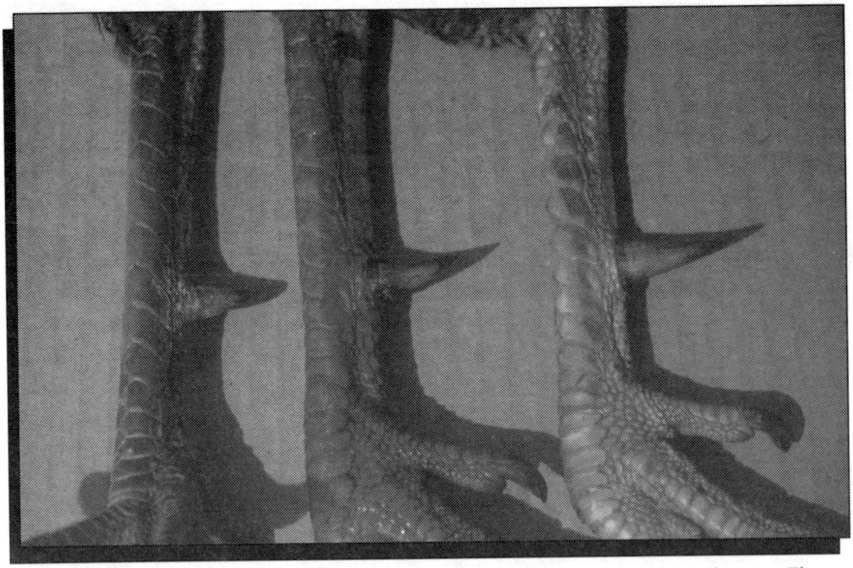

Spur length provides a somewhat reliable method for aging turkeys. These spurs are (l. to r.) from two, three and four-year-old toms.

Fans

One of the most striking characteristics of the wild turkey is its tail. The outer tail consists of 18 tail feathers, or retrices, that may be 12 to 18 inches long. When strutting, the gobbler will spread these feathers out, forming a fan. Toms can be easily distinguished from jakes by their fans. The tail feathers of a tom are of relatively even length throughout, and the fan then forms a perfect arc. Conversely, the central tail feathers of a jake are noticeably longer than the outside ones, appearing higher in the outstretched fan.

Sign

You can also sometimes use sign, like droppings and tracks, to tell the sex of the bird that left it. The feet of adult hens are smaller than those of adult males. In a track, the distance from the middle toe nail to the back of the heel is generally less than $4^{1/4}$ inches for hens, and often much longer for gobblers. They have different droppings too. Those of a hen are spiraled and bulbous, and look almost like a kernel of popped corn. The gobbler's are elongated and "L" or "J" shaped. Just remember: "J" for jake.

The tail fan of an adult gobbler contains feathers of relatively uniform length, while that of a jake will have several central feathers longer than the others, giving it an interrupted look.

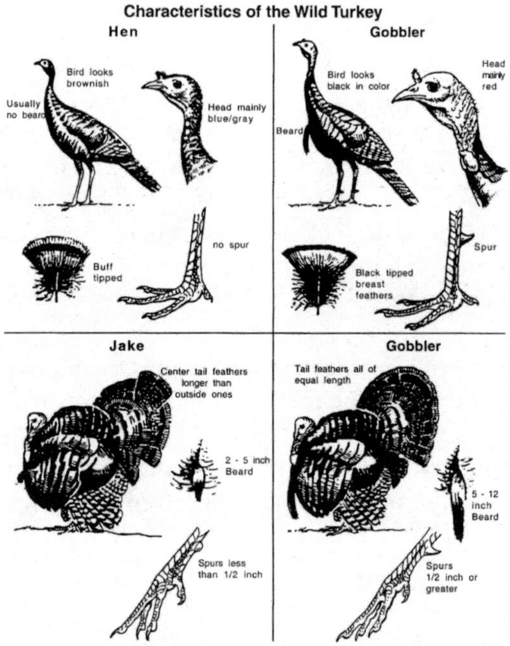

REPRINTED BY PERMISSION OF MAINE DEPARTMENT OF INLAND FISHERIES & WILDLIFE.

In spring, several behavioral characteristics help distinguish toms from hens. Toms strut as part of their mating ritual. When a gobbler goes into strut, he puffs out his body feathers, making him look much larger. He also fans out that remarkable tail, and lowers his wingtips so they are touching the ground. On bare ground, the wingtips will sometimes leave drag marks, and the long outer wing feathers, or primaries, on a bird that's been strutting are often worn.

While strutting, the tom may also perform a "vocalization," sometimes referred to as the "spit and drum." It begins with a sharp "chunk" or "spit" sound, followed by a deep, resonating "doooom," as air vibrates in the turkey's chest. Male turkeys also gobble (thus, the name: gobbler) to attract a mate, while hens do not. Neither characteristic is 100 percent reliable. I have observed strutting hens, and have spoken to one person who claims to have seen gobbling hens (I think I'd have to see that for myself before I believe it).

The wild turkey's keen vision is legendary. They can assimilate detail very quickly, and with a slight turn of the head have 360-degree visibility.

SEXUAL SIMILARITIES

Both sexes share several characteristics that evolved as means to detect and avoid predators. It is said that if turkeys could smell, you'd never kill them. That is because, while their sense of smell is rather poor, they more than make up for it with their keen eyesight and hearing. The turkey's eyesight is legendary, to which any veteran turkey hunter can attest. Rather than magnification, it is the rate at which they can assimilate detail, and their wide field of vision, which account for this. With eyes located on both sides of its head, a turkey can see in opposite directions simultaneously, and cover a field of view encompassing 300 degrees. Though they lack our telescopic vision, they can determine relative distances with a slight turn of the head, which also allows a 360-degree field of vision.

Their hearing is acute, as well. Studies suggest that they can hear in the subsonic and supersonic range, below and above the range in which humans hear. They also seem to be able to pinpoint the location of certain sounds. For instance, once you've yelped on a box call, that nearby gobbler seems to know precisely where you are. And if he's so inclined, he can come to your exact location. While this has yet to be proven scientifically, I've observed it enough times to believe it's true.

Wild turkeys have two other traits that they use to avoid danger. Running, particularly in heavy cover, is often their "preferred" mode of escape. Their powerful legs propel them up to 12 miles per hour, allowing them to easily out-distance a man (I speak from experience). They are also very strong flyers. Young turkeys, or "poults," can fly at eight to ten days of age, though only for short distances. Adults can fly continuously for roughly 200 yards, but can attain even longer distances by alternately flapping and gliding, sometimes reaching speeds of up to 55 miles per hour.

Now you know a little more about the wild turkey, at least the physical characteristics that distinguish the sexes, and that help both males and females avoid predators, and us. Hopefully, that is enough to pique your interest to learn more. To gain an even greater appreciation for what a remarkable bird the wild turkey is, you must next place it in the context of its environment. The next chapter will put you there and take you through the four seasons of the wild turkey.

two

FOUR SEASONS

two

If your goal is merely to be a successful turkey hunter, then you're primarily concerned with what goes on in the turkey's world in the spring and perhaps the fall. Spring hunting seasons in New England span most or all the month of May. And over those 31 days, turkeys go through many behavioral changes. Knowing when and why can help you choose the appropriate hunting tactics. In the fall, the turkey's behavior is markedly different than in the spring. It also changes from early to late fall. If you try to apply spring tactics in the fall, or early fall techniques in late fall, you'll likely end up frustrated and confused. In either case, spring or fall, knowing more about the turkey's natural history and behavior during these respective seasons can help to make you a better and more successful hunter.

As already mentioned, the most consistently successful hunters are students of their quarry, and those same hunters know that summer and winter are just as important to the turkey's survival as they are to the education of the turkey hunter. Besides, if you're like me, you may judge the success of your hunts not so much on whether you killed a bird, but by what you got out of those hunts. If you are successful in killing a bird, that success is all the more rewarding if you have a better understanding of what remarkable creatures these wild turkeys are. But to do so, you need to spend an entire year with them.

To live in New England, you have to be adaptable; and wild turkeys are certainly that. Not only are they well adapted to living in the wild, they can thrive in habitats as diverse as the remote woodlands of central Maine and the suburban woodlots of southern Connecticut. They have learned not only how to live among humans, but to thrive there, exploiting silage piles and bird feeders. Yet they are also masters of avoiding humans when they want to. They can tolerate a tremendous range of seasonal and climatic conditions. But to do so, they must

Winter is a critical period for turkeys—a bottleneck of survival. This is when food supplies are at their greatest scarcity and weather conditions are most severe.

annually shift their diet, habitat and behavior in response to varying environmental and physiological changes that take place over the course of a year.

WINTER

We begin our discussion of the annual life cycle of the turkey with winter. This is a critical period for turkeys in New England—a bottleneck of survival. Weather can be severe, with deep snow and bone-chilling temperatures that may plunge well below freezing. This is a time when food is least abundant and available. There is no greenery and much of the available mast, such as fruits and nuts, has already been gleaned from the forest floor by deer, squirrels and the turkeys themselves, as they fattened up for the coming winter. What little food remains is often sequestered under a blanket of snow and ice.

Snow depth and consistency are particularly critical to the turkey's survival. Shallow powder presents little difficulty, as turkeys can easily move about and scratch through it to find food beneath. Deep snow, especially powder, impedes turkey movement, making it more difficult for them to get to food. Conversely, a firm crust affords greater mobil-

Turkeys often rely on dairy farms for their winter survival. Large flocks will concentrate on the farms where they can feed on waste grain and silage.

ity, but makes food harder to get at. Food will remain scarce through the winter, until the late winter sun begins warming the south-facing hillsides, where turkeys will first begin to wander away from their winter concentration areas. But let's not get ahead of ourselves.

Daily activity is rather slow in winter, and consists largely of moving from roosting to feeding areas. During extremely cold periods, turkeys may not leave the roost until later in the morning, and may spend considerable time during midday periods just loafing. During storms, they may not leave at all. Prolonged storms with heavy snowfall can even result in turkeys starving to death on the roost.

Fortunately, turkeys have an unwitting ally. Throughout much of New England, particularly the northern states, turkeys rely heavily on dairy farms. Just as deer migrate to traditional wintering areas, turkeys may travel ten miles or more to winter on farms they first visited while still in the company of their mother hen. There, large winter congregations can often be found picking grain from silage piles, which is why biologists often choose these places for their release sights. In more developed areas, turkeys are becoming increasingly more common at backyard bird feeders, too.

In winter, turkeys are very social and large winter flocks often contain hens and jennies (yearling hens), toms and jakes. Birds become much more tolerant of one another as pecking orders, established during the summer and fall, are loosened. However, as the days begin to

The social organization of turkey flocks is governed by a linear dominance hierarchy or "pecking order," wherein each bird dominates those of lesser social rank. As the breeding season progresses, fights often break out between rival males.

grow longer toward the end of winter, changes begin to take place in the social structure of the flock.

SPRING

The turkey's spring begins long before ours. The onset of their mating season is one of the first harbingers of spring, preceding even the arrival of the first robins and red-winged blackbirds to New England. To us, it still feels like winter; the trees are bare, and snow often blankets the ground. But it is day length, not temperature, that powers the turkey's biological clock. Sometimes as early as mid February, toms will begin gobbling from the roost and strutting among the large winter flocks. The change is very gradual, but as this behavior escalates, tempers begin to flare, particularly among the males.

The social organization of winter flocks is governed by a linear, dominance hierarchy or "pecking order," wherein each bird dominates those of lesser social rank. The alpha bird dominates all others, and the

A tom tries to attract a mate by gobbling. Gobbling is most intense early in the morning, and the sound can sometimes be heard from up to a mile away.

omega is dominated by all others. Males and females have separate pecking orders, and there are separate orders within and between same-sex flocks. The pecking order is maintained throughout the year, but fighting among males becomes more prevalent at the onset of the breeding season as rivals joust for position to ultimately determine who wins breeding rights. Jakes, meanwhile, are going through the same motions of establishing dominance, though few, if any, will have an opportunity to mate.

As the days grow longer, winter flocks begin to break up. Turkeys begin spreading out across the landscape and segregating into smaller groups of similar age and sex. Male flocks are typically composed of toms that were raised together in the same family flock, and individuals are often siblings. The alpha male within such a flock is sometimes referred to as the "boss tom." He will breed most of the hens in his area. However, toms are not strictly territorial, and will tolerate other males of the same age or younger. These subordinates are called "satellite toms."

While there are numerous exceptions and variations, the tom's mating routine is fairly ritualized. In a typical scenario, he begins at dawn by gobbling from the roost. This is a long-distance call designed to attract females. Shortly after light breaks, turkeys fly down from the roost. If alone, the tom may continue gobbling, often moving to an elevated position, from which the sound of his gobbling will travel farther. When toms are accompanied by hens however, gobbling often wanes and then ceases soon after the birds are on the ground. As the hens move off to feed, the tom follows along, strutting and drumming.

The mating display of the wild turkey is a magnificent promenade. The tom begins by erecting or puffing up his body feathers. He simultaneously lifts his tail perpendicular to the ground and spreads out his tail feathers to form a full-fan, as he spreads and lowers his wings so the outer primaries drag on the ground. The strutting tom looks both enormous and resplendent.

In this pose, he will take two or three quick steps, then utter a sharp "spit" sound followed by a low-pitched hum that seems to make him tremble. Not a true vocalization, the latter sound is produced by air resonating in the gobbler's chest

He will continue his display until a hen shows she is receptive to his advances. She does this by first holding her body horizontal and her neck flexed against her back, then by squatting on the ground. The tom will walk up on the squatting hen, treading on, or "kneading," her back with his feet, stimulating her to raise her tail so that mating can be accomplished.

Wild turkeys are polygynous, which means a gobbler will mate with as many hens as he can. Gobblers take no part in nesting or brood rearing, so once a tom has "finished his business," he can turn his attention immediately to another hen. Early in the mating season, before the hens are bred, they will travel together throughout the day, and the tom will remain with them.

Meanwhile, some of the subordinate males, or other satellites not associated with a gobbler group, may move off in search of their own harem. These subordinates and satellites, which are often two-year-old birds, comprise much of the early-season bag, and it is said they "make

The tom will walk up on the squatting hen, treading on or "kneading" her back with his feet, which stimulates her to raise her tail so that mating can be completed.

you feel like a turkey hunter." They gobble and strut just like the older birds, and have full fans and long beards and spurs, but are much more susceptible to calling. They provide the most willing targets for early-season hunters. From his years of experience in making hunting videos, Wil Primos, of Primos game calls, refers to these birds as "movie stars" because of their cooperative nature.

After mating, the hen gradually becomes more solitary. Eventually, she'll leave the flock to lay a single egg in a ground nest, which typically consists of little more than a shallow depression scratched out in the leaves and duff. She'll then cover the egg with leaves and return to the flock or move off on her own to feed. She will return a day or two later to lay a second egg, and may skip another day before laying a third. While there is considerable variation, hens usually sit for an average of about one hour after laying each of their first five eggs. After the sixth egg, they may remain two hours. Sitting time continues to increase by about an hour with the laying of each subsequent egg. At this time she is still roosting in trees at night. Once she has completed her clutch, which typically consists of ten to 12 eggs, she will incubate continuously, day and night, leaving the nest only for brief feeding recesses. Most

New England states set their hunting seasons to begin around this time to minimize disturbance to the nesting hens, and ensure most of the breeding has already occurred. This is also why legal hunting ceases around midday.

Toms, meanwhile, are still actively seeking hens. But as the hens begin falling out of the ranks, toms must travel farther and wider in search of a potential mate, making them more susceptible to hunters. This is enhanced by a second peak in gobbling, which occurs around the same time, often coinciding with the start of most New England turkey seasons.

While weather does not directly influence the timing of the breeding season, it can have a significant effect on the breeding status of individual birds, as can predators. Because hens do not begin incubating until their clutch is complete, the eggs are left unguarded for long periods. In an average spring, only about 35 to 40 percent of the nests will ever hatch, primarily due to adverse weather or predation.

If her nest is destroyed, the hen must start all over again. Some may re-nest, while others may simply give up. This depends on several factors, including how late into the nesting season they lose their clutch. While most hens should be incubating by mid to late May, in years with cold, rainy springs many may not. Furthermore, for reasons not well understood, not all hens breed, and some may remain with the breeding flock throughout the spring hunting season.

Once her clutch is complete, a hen will remain on her nest most of the day, leaving only for short feeding bouts lasting perhaps an hour or two, and sometimes skipping a day of feeding altogether. The average incubation period is 26 to 28 days. All of the chicks will hatch within 12 to 24 hours. Young turkeys, or poults, are precocial, which means they hatch with eyes open, and as soon as their downy feathers dry they will be ready to leave the nest. While hatching dates vary from year to year, and on a north-south gradient, most clutches hatch around the first week of June in New England.

SUMMER

Summer is the time of plenty: plenty of birds and plenty of food. There are also plenty of pitfalls. Turkey populations are at their most abundant just after the hatching period. However, only about 25 to 50 percent of the young will survive until the fall. Predators such as foxes, coyotes, goshawks and great-horned owls will take a heavy toll. Still, one of the greatest killers of poults is weather. The poorly-feathered young birds are highly susceptible to hypothermia (exposure), and extended periods of cold spring rains can be disastrous.

When the poults are between three and eight weeks of age, hens and their broods begin combining with other brood flocks to form larger assemblages. They may remain together for some time, or capriciously go their separate ways. At this time, turkeys spend most of their waking hours feeding.

Wild turkeys feed on a variety of plants and insects. Plants may make up as much as 85 percent of the adult's diet while the opposite is true for poults. The young rely much more heavily on a protein-rich diet of insects to power their rapidly-growing bodies. As they mature, their diet gradually shifts from insects to succulent plants. Later, the diets of both young and mature birds begins to shift again as seeds, nuts and berries ripen. As the days begin to grow shorter, they rely more heavily on the high-calorie content of these foods, which they'll need to fatten up for the winter.

FALL

Fall is a time of relative stability among turkey flocks. Pecking orders have been established, and young birds now behave more like adults. About the only major change that occurs is a gradual shift from summer to fall range, which usually consists of moving from field to forest habitat. Here, turkeys will find their most important fall food: hard mast. Acorns and beechnuts make up a significant portion of the turkey's fall diet, except in areas where they have access to post-harvest waste grains like corn. They will also visit freshly-plowed fields to pick unearthed insects, or fields spread with manure, where they can find seeds and undigested gain.

Turkeys begin the fall wandering in search of food. Once a flock finds a reliable food source, they will often remain in close proximity for as long as it lasts, particularly if mast is scarce. Conversely, if mast is widespread and abundant, they may range farther, and their daily movements will be less predictable. Eventually, as the mercury drops and the woods change from brown to white, brood flocks, gobblers and jakes begin to coalesce into larger winter assemblages, and the annual cycle begins anew.

In fall, turkeys will often form large brood flocks consisting of several hens and their offspring.

The wild turkey is truly a marvel of nature, adaptable and complex. We are blessed to have such a proud symbol of American wilderness living amongst us in such great numbers. However, our appreciation of the turkey becomes even greater when you consider that there was a time, not so long ago, when the king of game birds was entirely absent from our region.

three

RETURN OF THE THANKSGIVING BIRD

three

For anyone who has traveled the highways or back roads of New England in recent years, and for New England turkey hunters especially, it is hard to imagine there was a time, not so long ago, when turkeys were virtually nonexistent across our six-state region. In my own lifetime, I have seen them restored to huntable numbers in all six states. This is one of the most remarkable success stories in modern conservation, and much of that success is directly attributable to hunters.

We were the first conservationists, the ones to call upon state fish and game agencies and ask for reintroduction programs, and the ones to fund those programs through the sale of hunting licenses and through private organizations like the National Wild Turkey Federation. And now, we are the ones to reap the benefits. Thus, it behooves us to know and understand not only the natural history, but the history of this great bird we pursue. Only then can we fully appreciate what a wonderful opportunity turkey hunting provides. That is why I have included this chapter and the next.

The wild turkey is symbolic of many things. To many people it represents Thanksgiving and sustenance provided by the New World to the first permanent European settlement in Plymouth, Massachusetts. It is also a symbol of our country and our continent. Its red, white and blue head coincidentally displays the colors of our flag. Indigenous to North America, it is the only important domestic animal to originate in the western hemisphere. And though its cousins have been domesticated into dull-witted, lethargic creatures, the true wild turkey remains a symbol of wilderness, much as those of us who hunt distinguish ourselves from those who don't.

The wild turkey also exemplifies the history of conservation in North America. Turkeys were seemingly abundant beyond limit at the time of the first Thanksgiving. But with expanded settlement of the Eastern Seaboard came deforestation and a flourishing wild game mar-

Indigenous to North America, wild and wary, brought back from the brink of extinction and now flourishing, the wild turkey is symbolic of our country and our continent in so many ways.

ket. Less than three centuries later, turkeys were gone, extirpated from much of their former range in the eastern United States. The last recorded wild turkey in Massachusetts was on Mount Tom, in 1851, and for a long time the wild turkey was absent from the land of the pilgrims.

Modern conservationists-hunters sought to rectify that, however, and thanks to the efforts of biologists and volunteers, generously supported by hunters' dollars, New England's wild turkeys were brought back from the brink. Local success stories abound, but perhaps the most historically symbolic occurred when the 2000 Massachusetts spring turkey season opened. The area open to hunting was expanded to include Plymouth County for the first time in modern history. Nimrods could once again challenge the king of North American game birds in a place where the last turkey hunters probably toted flintlock muskets and wore tri-corner hats. We had come full circle; the Thanksgiving bird had returned.

After several failed attempts at introducing farm-raised birds, biologists began to experience success by trapping and relocating wild birds. The National Wild Turkey Federation and its many local chapters have been invaluable to turkey restoration efforts, providing funding, materials and volunteer labor to state's efforts.

REINTRODUCTION

According to biologists I've spoken with, wild turkeys now occur in numbers that probably never existed before in our region, and occupy a geographic area that certainly far exceeds their historic range. Getting to this point, however, did not come easy. Lack of knowledge and proper funding misdirected or stalled some early efforts, in some cases for decades. Other factors, such as poor weather and the turkey's prerogative to travel, also hindered some relocation efforts.

THE EARLY YEARS

The story of turkey restoration in the northeast is similar to that from other parts of the country. It began with sportsmen's requests to their state fish and game agencies. The first attempts at stocking game-farm birds were unsuccessful because those early strains were poorly equipped to survive in the wild, and soon died out. Restoration programs floundered for several decades, until biologists discovered they could successfully relocate wild birds to new range. In the Northeast, the first trap and transfer of wild birds occurred in New York and Pennsylvania. The fruits of those successes were, in turn, seed stock for New England's restoration efforts.

Appropriately perhaps, Massachusetts residents were pioneers in these efforts. Private individuals stocked the first wild birds, of unknown origin, on Naushon Island in 1922 and 1923. According to Division of Fisheries and Wildlife biologist Jim Cardoza, however, numerous other efforts prior to the early 1970s were largely unsuccessful, as they too relied on captive-raised birds.

The Vermont Fish and Wildlife Department began their first relocations during the winter of 1969, when 17 wild birds trapped in New York were released in Pawlet, which lies in southern Vermont, near the New York border. Among those involved in that project was a young game warden named Stu Bristol, who would later become one of the most recognized turkey hunting figures in New England. Results were quick in coming, and hens with broods were sighted the following spring. The next winter, 14 more New York birds were transplanted to nearby Hubbardton. More transplants occurred and within two years, breeding populations were established along the Vermont and New York border. From that point on Vermont's turkey program was autonomous, relying on in-state trap and transfer. Initially, the Department expected the population would be limited to its historic range, roughly south of US Route 4. Turkeys would eventually far exceed those limits.

The next ten or so years were quite productive for turkey restoration throughout New England. Seeing Vermont's success, other states followed suit. In 1972 and 1973, Massachusetts released 37 wild-trapped New York birds in Beartown State Forest in the southern Berkshires. Once established, those flocks became the core of the Bay State's turkey population and subsequent relocation efforts. In 1973, Vermont held its first modern turkey season, in parts of Addision, Bennington and Rutland Counties, and 23 of the 579 hunters issued permits were successful.

Once turkey populations were well-established, several states began expanding hunting opportunities to the fall.

Fall hunting began in the Green Mountain State just two years later, in 1975, in a limited area of southwestern Vermont. That same year, both Connecticut and New Hampshire saw their first releases of wild-caught birds, also from New York. While New Hampshire's early efforts were hampered by limited financial support, Connecticut's program flourished. Its proximity to New York helped, as birds translocated within the Empire State often wandered across the border. By 1977, Connecticut biologists were trapping and relocating birds within their state and by decade's end, turkey distribution was nearly statewide.

Seeing successful reintroduction efforts in nearby Vermont and New Hampshire during the 1970s, the Maine Department of Inland Fisheries & Wildlife responded to sportsmen's requests and began their restoration program. Biologist Phil Bozenhard orchestrated some of the first intra-New England translocations, releasing birds from Vermont and Connecticut into the Mount Agamenticus area of southernmost York County in 1977 and 1978. Results were slow in coming. With limited funds and staffing, further releases were stalled. Meanwhile, a portion of Maine's flock relocated itself into New Hampshire.

By decade's end, Bay State biologists began live trapping birds from the Berkshires and transplanting them within the State, and in 1980, wild turkeys became legal game in Massachusetts for the first time since 1851. Though I was fortunate enough to be among the 1,250 permitees in that historic hunt, I was not among the 72 who were successful. The beginning of the 1980s also saw Rhode Island release their first flock of wild birds, in Exeter. These birds were live-trapped and translocated from Pawlet, Vermont—site of the first Vermont release. They also benefitted from nomadic Connecticut birds released just over the state line in 1983 and 1984. Population growth was initially slow, and another 14 years would lapse before the next releases in Rhode Island.

Meanwhile, things were going much better next door, and Connecticut's first modern spring season occurred in 1981. Vermont abandoned limiting permit numbers and added a late December hunt to their fall season the same year, and Maine's program was getting back on track. Invigorated by help from the newly formed Maine chapter of the National Wild Turkey Federation, they began live-trapping York County birds and relocating them elsewhere in the state. They also continued releasing Connecticut birds at various locations.

MIDDLE AGE

The 1980s saw a similar trend throughout the region with both turkey populations and hunting opportunities expanding, in many cases beyond the expectations of biologists. Vermont's harvest remained around 200 to 300 birds until 1983, when it began to climb steadily. Vermont continued to relocate birds within the state, as well as supply other states, provinces, and countries.

In 1985, New Hampshire established their first fall turkey season. Designed to provide the maximum opportunity with the least impact, the archery-only season now runs a full three months, concurrent with the archery season for deer. In 1986, both Maine and Rhode Island held their first spring seasons, making wild turkeys legal game in all six New England States. Rhode Islander's started first, on May 5, taking eight gobblers. Of the 500 permitees who hunted Maine's inaugural season on May 8, nine eventually bagged birds. Progress remained steady through the end of the decade.

Massachusetts began the next decade with their first fall season, in 1990. Hunting was limited to roughly the western third of the state until 1997, when the zone was expanded eastward to include most of the State's western half. That same year, the spring season was extended by a week, and expanded east to include Essex and Middlesex Counties.

Reintroduction efforts have been so successful that several states now offer multi-bird limits in the spring.

Throughout the 1990s, Maine continued to release birds at new locations, relying more on resident birds in the latter years. The program was originally designed to reestablish turkeys in their historical range along the southern coast. However, encouraged by their repeated success, biologists transplanted birds farther inland and north, beyond the limits of anyone's expectations. It worked. In 1996, the area open to hunting was again expanded to include most of the bird's current range in Maine, extending north and east from the New Hampshire border to the Penobscot River, and encompassing seven counties.

From 1994 through 1996, Rhode Island released 108 turkeys at six sites in Burrillville, Foster, Little Compton, Scituate, Tiverton and West Greenwich. That was just the trick; birds expanded and harvest rates, which had been stable and low, began to climb rapidly. According to biologist Brian Tefft, the offspring of those birds now occupy nearly all of the approximately 500 square miles of suitable habitat in the state.

THE RECENT PAST AND PRESENT

As turkey populations and hunting opportunities continued to expand, record harvests became the trend in most New England states. In 1998 Vermonters experienced a record spring harvest of 2,450 birds, and biologist Doug Blodgett estimated the State's turkey population at approximately 25,000. New Hampshire hunters also established a new harvest record in 1998, in the process topping 1,000 for the first time since birds were re-introduced. This was an astounding 34 percent increase over the previous year. Maine hunters experienced their fifth consecutive record year in 1998, bagging 594 birds, and Maine's turkey population was estimated at around 8,000, and expanding in both number and area. Rhode Island hunters continued their record-breaking trend as well, topping 100 for the first time, more than a 50 percent increase over 1997. The only signs of leveling off came from Connecticut, where biologist Mike Gregonis observed their turkey harvest had been relatively stable for several years in a row.

The following year, 1999, all six states set new spring kill records. Vermont's kill increased by nearly 30 percent over the previous year, New Hampshire's increased by more than 34 percent, and Maine's was more than 50 percent higher. Phil Bozenhard attributed this success to two factors: "People are learning how to hunt turkeys in Maine, and there are a lot of turkeys around." It also didn't hurt that they had more permits and more area to hunt.

By 1999, Jim Cardoza estimated the Bay State turkey population at somewhere between 15,000 and 18,000 and said, "Turkeys have been successfully introduced everywhere it's practical to have them." That year, MassWildlife eliminated the split season, allowing all hunters to hunt throughout the entire four-week season. Also, hunters formerly restricted to taking one bird in the spring and one in the fall could opt to take both birds in the spring. Finally, the area open to spring hunting was expanded to include Barnstable, Bristol and Norfolk Counties, and Plymouth County.

In 2000, Maine, New Hampshire and Vermont all experienced record kills of 1,521, 1,832 and 3,818 birds, respectively. Rhode Island's take was identical to the previous year (147), and Massachusetts had their second highest kill on record (2,147). Maine again increased the number of available permits, this time from 3,000 to 4,000. That year saw a cold, wet spring followed by a late, severe winter.

With poor nesting conditions in the spring of 2000, biologists anticipated a drop in the 2001 kill. The resilient turkeys proved them mostly wrong, once again. Hunters bagged 2,259 gobblers in the Granite State, a 20 percent increase over the 2000 kill, and an unexpected jump over the predicted harvest of between 1,500 and 1,800 gobblers. Connecticut's reported take of 2,067 birds also set yet another record. Rhode Island issued 311 more permits, resulting in a record kill of 207 birds, and turkeys were harvested in 19 of Rhode Island's 39 towns. Maine increased permit numbers to 7,000, went to a split season, limiting 3,500 permit holders to each of the two-week segments, and set a new record of 2,544, second highest in New England. In Vermont, the perennial frontrunner, Green Mountain hunters not only set a new record but did so handily, with 4,626 birds. Doug Blodgett estimated the state's population in the neighborhood of 35,000 turkeys, which is a nice neighborhood. Jim Cardoza was also pleasantly surprised by the Bay State's 2,163-bird kill. "Given the poor hatch during last year's nesting season and the severe winter we had over much of the state, I didn't expect a near record kill. I think the excellent hunting conditions we had this spring, particularly during the first week of the season, really contributed to hunter success."

In 2002, Maine increased the number of available spring permits from 7,000 to 9,000, went to a five-week split season, and set a new record of 3,391 birds. They then followed New Hampshire's example by holding their first archery-only fall season. Rhode Island increased the number of permits issued from 1,311 to 1,456 and experienced yet another record kill of 256 birds. New Hampshire's record total of 2,597 was expected, while a six percent decline to 2,026 in Massachusetts was no surprise, given the poor weather conditions.

While biologists contend that the rate of increase in turkey populations and annual harvest have slowed, both continue to rise just about annually, even under the worst conditions. Hunting opportunities also continue to increase, particularly in the three northern states, where turkey populations still have room to expand. With the bulk of restoration efforts complete, biologists can now turn their attention to other matters, such as monitoring populations, improving habitat and maintaining or increasing access, which we'll cover in the next chapter.

four

ONGOING MANAGEMENT EFFORTS

four

While restoration efforts throughout New England have been deemed an overwhelming success, there is still much to be done. Biologists and managers throughout the region are constantly looking for ways to expand hunting opportunities within the turkey population strongholds and increase populations along the fringes. Meanwhile, in some areas turkey populations are even approaching nuisance levels and need to be dealt with. State agencies, assisted by funding and support from the various local chapters of the National Wild Turkey Federation, are also developing and implementing habitat improvement projects to ensure the viability of existing populations. Perhaps the greatest threat to the future of turkey hunting is urban sprawl and ever-diminishing access to private land. What follows is a state-of-the-state summary of ongoing turkey management.

MAINE

Maine's turkey population and management programs have reached middle age. That is to say, the initial growth stage is over, but there are still holes to be filled. Regional wildlife biologist Phil Bozenhard identified 1999 as a turning point. Up to that point, Maine's turkey population had been experiencing slow, steady growth. Since then it has skyrocketed. "The birds reached critical mass," he said. "We had a favorable spring with warm, dry conditions, which led to nearly 80 percent survival rate of poults. There were birds everywhere, and that was when the population got ahead of hunters."

In 1985, biologists estimated Maine's turkey population at less than 900 birds. By 2000, Bozenhard conservatively estimated the population had risen to approximately 10,000, and that the statewide maximum supportable population was around 15,000 birds, based on available habitat. Just two years later, however, biologist Andy Weik estimated the statewide population at somewhere between 17,000 and 20,000 birds, and growing. "Now, we've got birds everywhere, from Kittery to Brownfield, north to Bangor and back," said Bozenhard.

When will the population explosion end? Very likely, it will be soon. Maine has taken a very conservative approach with regard to its hunting seasons. From the beginning, spring hunting permits have been given out on a lottery basis. Concurrently, demand has almost always exceeded the supply of available permits, despite annual increases in permit numbers since 1995. The number of applicants increased, from a little

Maine's turkey populations experienced slow growth for a number of years, but once it reached "critical mass" the birds took off. Healthy populations now occur in areas once thought unsuitable by biologists.

over 18,000 in 2001 to nearly 26,000 in 2002. Initially, permit numbers were limited, to give the birds a chance to get established. More recently, the Department has limited permits to preserve the safety and the quality of the hunt.

Since the beginning of this century, however (and actually some time before), it has become clear there is no longer a biological need to limit numbers of spring hunters. In 2001, the Department issued 7,000 permits and hunters killed 2,517 birds. In 2002, 9,000 permitted hunters killed 3,391 birds. Clearly, hunting is not limiting population growth, yet.

In the fall of 2002 Maine experienced their first either-sex fall season, limited to bowhunting only. Because they are for either sex, fall seasons tend to have a greater impact on turkey population growth, except in the case of archery-only restrictions. However, if turkey population growth continues, muzzleloader or shotgun hunting may eventually be added to the fall season. Furthermore, Maine will likely see an end to the spring lottery permit system soon. Meanwhile, the Department continues to relocate birds within the state to fill in gaps between established populations.

In April of 2000, the Department convened a public Wild Turkey Working Group. Their charge was to develop goals and objectives to guide wild turkey management for the ensuing ten to 15 years. The overriding goal recommended by the group was to increase the wild turkey population within all suitable habitat in Maine. Under this goal they set five specific objectives:

1) By 2010, increase the size and distribution of the wild turkey population within all suitable habitat in Maine via trap and transfer activities and habitat improvements.

2) By 2010, provide unlimited spring hunting opportunity, as long as the wild turkey population can support it and current (2000) hunt quality is maintained. Among the issues still to be addressed were how to expand hunter education and how to define "quality hunting."

3) By 2002, develop a component to the Department's Nuisance Wildlife Policy that addresses wild turkeys. Several issues were raised about nuisance complaints, damage, and depredation permits, and the Department is addressing these.

4) By 2003, implement a limited fall season in areas where the wild turkey population can support it, without adversely affecting Objective 2. The Department has acknowledged that this will require better knowledge of the population status and will require a law change.

5) Develop a cooperative habitat improvement program between landowners, the Maine chapter of the National Wild Turkey Federation, and the Department.

Another principal concern among group members was finding and ensuring adequate funding to support a new position whose responsibility is to coordinate wild turkey management. Somewhat of an afterthought, participants unanimously agreed this was critical to proper management of this growing resource and hunting opportunity.

NEW HAMPSHIRE

In 1990, biologist Ted Walski set a statewide population goal of 4,000 to 5,000 turkeys. More recently, he recalled a time when he felt the population would never reach 10,000. In August 2002, however, he estimated the population at 23,000. According to Walski, turkeys now occur in all ten counties, with the greatest numbers in the western half of the state: Cheshire, Sullivan and Grafton Counties. But Walski expects that South-Central counties like Hillsboro, Merrimack and Carroll may end up surpassing some of that in a year or so.

Having far surpassed early population goals, the New Hampshire Fish & Game Department is now taking a closer look at population dynamics and exploring ways to expand hunting opportunities. In 2002, a team of five biologist met to formulate future management plans. Among the things they considered were allowing a second spring gobbler by archery, opening the remainder of Coos County to spring hunting, a youth turkey hunt and fall shotgun season. The biologists felt that New Hampshire's turkey population is already experiencing considerable hunting pressure. The majority of wildlife management units have growing turkey populations well below carrying capacity, and densities of gobblers per square mile in the spring harvest are considerably below units in neighboring Vermont.

With that in mind, they recommended no fall shotgun season or second spring gobbler by bow. "Looking at turkey kill density, there are only a handful of towns where hunters are taking at least one gobbler per square mile in the spring," said Walski. "That's kind of a yardstick as to when you can begin thinking about a fall (shotgun) season. Before you start a fall season you better make sure you have enough birds. Let's not shoot the goose that lays the golden egg."

They did suggest several new opportunities. Though they have some concerns over the impact on breeding and nesting, and fairness to other hunters, they recommended a one or two-day youth hunt immediately prior to the regular spring opening. They also recommended opening remaining towns in Coos County to spring hunting, and suggested a one-week season. In conjunction with this, they recommended trapping and banding gobblers in Coos County to gain information on harvest rates and survival.

Thanks to the efforts of dedicated biologists like Ted Walski, shown here checking in a bird, the Granite State's turkey population is flourishing in southern and central parts of the state and still growing up north.

The team also revisited a couple of old ideas. The Department mailed out turkey hunter questionnaires from 1980 to 1989 to gather information on where persons hunted, the degree of contact with turkeys, degree of hunting conflict, hunting pressure, type of firearms and ammunition used, days hunted, etc. Maine has done so annually since the beginning of their turkey hunt, and uses this information to guide future management. New Hampshire biologists felt it was time to begin this again in their state.

The last time New Hampshire prepared a long-term management plan was in 1990, and it was intended as a five-year plan. Biologists felt it was time to bring this plan up to date and design it for future management.

In 2001 and 2002, they conducted two studies. One involved determining the seasonal home range of turkeys causing agricultural damage in the upper Connecticut River valley, and the reproductive ecology of nesting hens in western Grafton County. The other involved researching the metabolic rates of free-ranging wild turkeys. Both studies are ongoing and results are pending.

Walski noted the Department faces several challenges to future management. One is habitat. "New Hampshire doesn't have extensive farmland. This limits both habitat and hunting opportunity, and often leads to too much [hunting] pressure on popular spots. It's also a key to winter survival and brood habitat. There's not much you can do with less than 200 dairy farms in ten counties," he says. "Bird feeders are a key element in winter." Studies of radio-collared birds have shown that close to 100 percent are nesting within a few hundred feet of the edge of a field or pasture "Where there's no farmland left, we need to keep some kind of pasture or field as it's important brood habitat."

VERMONT

Vermont's turkey population hit a peak of between 9,000 and 12,000 birds in the late 1980s. This was followed by the severe winter of 1993-1994, when it was estimated as much as 50 percent of the population may have perished. Emergency hunting regulations were implemented to reduce spring and fall harvest and allow the population to recover. With these conservative measures, and a string of favorable spring nesting conditions and mild winters, the population rebounded rapidly, and is now estimated at between 23,000 and 24,000 birds.

In 1999, the Vermont Department of Fish & Wildlife prepared a ten-year plan to protect, conserve and manage wild turkeys for the people of Vermont. This was based both on biologist's recommendations and those of the general public. Currently, hunting of some form is allowed in about two-thirds of the state. The Department hopes to increase opportunities where they currently exist, and expand them to some areas where they do not.

As their overriding goal is to maintain sustainable populations, the Department first established threshold criteria as a guideline to when they could or should initiate, liberalize or curtail spring and fall hunting opportunities. Since then, they have expanded the spring hunting zone to include several new areas.

Given the disparity of habitat in different parts of the state, the Department is also considering adopting turkey hunting season zones based on existing wildlife management units. This would give them better control over localized populations. They have also proposed reducing the length of the fall shotgun season in areas that have lower population densities, lesser habitat quality and greater winter severity. In the long run, this would ultimately increase the quality of both the fall and spring hunts in these areas.

MASSACHUSETTS

According to MassWildlife turkey project leader Jim Cardoza, the Division's initial goal was to restore turkeys to all suitable range in the state. "We've worked hard to restore the wild turkey across the Commonwealth," he says. That goal was met in 1996, when the trap and transplant program was completed. "Now we're seeing the fruits of those labors in the form of a thriving turkey population that's enjoyed by sportsmen and the general public alike."

By 1996, turkeys could be found in Massachusetts just about everywhere from Worcester County west, except in the metropolitan areas of Springfield and Worcester. Now, good populations are also found in suitable, but more fragmented, habitats in Bristol, Essex, Middlesex, and Plymouth Counties. "It's particularly gratifying to see these great birds return to Plymouth County," said Cardoza, "where their importance as a wildlife resource is synonymous with the pilgrims." Turkeys are absent only from Nantucket and Suffolk Counties.

A second goal was to "initiate and expand, where practical, turkey hunting opportunities." They initiated spring hunting in 1980, and fall hunting in 1990. Since 1980, MassWildlife has limited hunting to a permit-only system, to keep hunter density at an optimum low level, ensuring a quality hunting experience and avoiding over-exploitation of the resource. It must be working because with eleven counties now open to spring hunting, virtually all hunters who apply are successful in getting a permit. Meanwhile, the turkey population continues to expand. "In 2003, that goal will essentially be finalized, as we will have all foreseeable hunting opportunities in place," says Cardoza. "We will have spring hunting allowed in 13 of the 14 deer zones (no habitat in Zone 14), of which a four-week season will prevail in 11 zones and a two-week season in two zones. Fall hunting will be allowed in ten

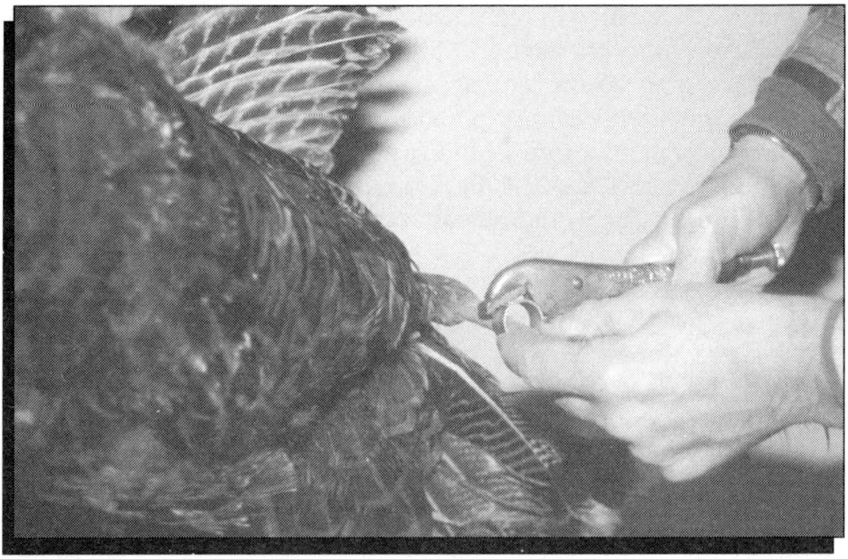

By banding captured birds, biologists can track their movements as well as monitor population growth.

zones; the remaining zones will probably never have sufficient populations to sustain fall hunting (at least firearms fall hunting).

The average statewide fall turkey population is about 18,000 to 20,000 birds. To keep tabs on the population, MassWildlife conducts a wild turkey brood survey each summer, from June through August. This is to aid in estimating poult production and survival. They rely on reports from knowledgeable cooperators to obtain a large sample for this survey. No major changes are in store, though more areas may be opened to hunting during the various seasons as the population continues to expand.

The immediate future looks bright for both turkeys and turkey hunters in the Bay State.

"In the short term—ten years or so—turkeys should do just fine," says Cardoza. "In the long term—50 years or so—however, the future for turkeys and indeed much other wildlife is rather uncertain." Cardoza sees the greatest future management challenges coming as a direct or indirect result of human population growth and movement. "Human demands for space for residential and industrial facilities, transportation networks, and food production, stemming from the burgeoning human population, will continue to eliminate or fragment habitats for fish and wildlife, with increasing isolation of these populations, and consequent risk of local extinctions and loss of genetic diversity. Human population centers have shifted from rural areas to urban areas, with a consequent loss of ties to, and understanding of, the land. Consequently, we are losing our naturalists and our sportsmen, and that translates not only into a lack or participation, but an unreasoned and unreasoning antipathy to outdoor activities."

CONNECTICUT

Connecticut manages its turkey population, now estimated at over 30,000 birds, at levels compatible with available habitat and land uses, and to allow for a sustained yield, which provides recreational opportunities for sportsmen. They do this largely by establishing a variety of seasons and bag limits for spring and fall, and public and private land. By monitoring harvest trends and conducting research, they can ensure the long-term viability of the turkey population.

Connecticut has probably been the most aggressive New England state with regard to conducting research on their turkeys. Between 1975 and 1998, the Department of Environmental Protection (DEP) Wildlife Division and their cooperators undertook several studies to gain better insight into behavior, population dynamics and ecology of turkeys in the Nutmeg State. These studies were designed to monitor population growth, annual production rates and hunting mortality. Results were then used to set bag limits and season lengths, and to better understand turkey population dynamics.

In the 1970s and 1980s, the DEP distributed turkey sighting cards to interested volunteer cooperators to report sightings. These cards were used primarily to document range expansion and hen to poult ratios. Two side effects are that they also increased public awareness and encouraged public participation in Connecticut's turkey management program.

From 1984 to 1988, biologists conducted spring gobble counts to determine peak gobbling periods. Traveling predetermined ten-mile routes, they stopped every 0.8 mile and recorded gobbling activity. They then used this information to establish spring hunting season dates. Setting the spring season to coincide with the second peak of gobbling ensures that hens are least likely to come into contact with hunters and most of the breeding has already occurred.

From 1984 to 1986 the Wildlife Division and the University of Connecticut conducted a parasite survey. They collected viscera from turkeys brought to hunter check stations, then examined them for internal parasites and lesions. Though parasites were found, none were found to be harmful to turkeys or humans, and the DEP concluded Connecticut's turkey population was healthy.

In 1995, the Wildlife Division, NWTF, the University of Maine and Wildlife Forever initiated a two-year study to examine nesting ecology of southern Connecticut turkeys. Much of the incentive for this study was the development and forest fragmentation in this part of the state, which can lead to higher predation. As expected, results showed that human-induced land changes may negatively affect both productivity and population growth.

From 1996 to 1999, researchers used radio telemetry to monitor seasonal home ranges of hen turkeys. One noteworthy finding was that turkeys shifted toward farmland in winter to gain access to waste corn and silage, which become increasingly important during years of poor acorn production. In 1996, the Division also examined roosting habitat, and found that birds preferred habitat that minimized heat loss, especially during the winter. This included south-facing slopes, areas protected from prevailing winds and dense softwood stands.

Because roughly 80 percent of the state's land is privately owned, management is sometimes difficult. The Wildlife Division continues to monitor and document nuisance complaints in an effort to alleviate human-wildlife conflicts. They have also developed specific habitat management recommendations for private landowners who wish to maintain or improve turkey habitat.

RHODE ISLAND

The six-state New England region is a remarkably diverse one. This is perhaps most evident when you compare Rhode Island to Maine. The breadth of New England's largest state spans several ecological regions from the coniferous forests of the north to the transition forests of the south, and contains several counties equal to or larger than the entire state of Rhode Island. Ironically, the history and current status of wild turkey management are remarkably similar in both states. Both held their first modern spring seasons in the same year. They are the only two New England states that, as of this writing, still have a lottery permit system where applicants exceed the number of available permits.

And in both states, birds continue to colonize areas once thought to be unsuitable, though for different reasons.

According to Brian Tefft, principal wildlife biologist for the Rhode Island Department of Environmental Management's Division of Fish & Wildlife, the Ocean State's turkey population now stands at around 5,000 birds and growing. Turkeys have been reported in 25 of Rhode Island's 39 towns, and continue to expand into areas no one thought possible. Restoration efforts, according to Tefft, have been completed, as birds now occupy most areas of suitable habitat. Populations are still below carrying capacity in some areas, but with proper management are expected to reach, and perhaps exceed, those levels.

Management efforts are now directed toward monitoring the population and identifying needs and limiting factors, as well as managing the hunting season to ensure a sustained yield for sportsmen, and continued enjoyment by non-hunters. Agency personnel and landowner cooperators annually conduct brood surveys, where they record all sightings of hens with broods. The Division also conducts annual gobble counts, in much the same way as Connecticut. In addition, agency personnel also conduct mast surveys, where they record the relative abundance of hard mast (acorns) throughout the state. Results are then incorporated into management plans that include permit quotas for the ensuing seasons.

CONCLUSION

The future for turkeys and turkey hunting in New England looks remarkably bright. There is little question that with careful management, turkeys will continue to expand in both range and number. The greatest challenge for the future is ensuring that those turkeys will continue to be available as a harvestable resource for sportsmen. That means securing and improving access. While state fish and wildlife agencies continue to do their part, the onus ultimately rest squarely on the hunter's shoulders. Only by demonstrating ethical and responsible behavior and promoting our sport will we be able to ensure this tremendous resource will remain available for future generations.

five

CLOTHING

five

As I listened to the opening day weather forecast, my heart sank: "Heavy rain and blustery winds moving in overnight, tapering to showers by late morning." The best I could hope for was that the tapering would occur a little earlier than expected. Given those conditions, a good many casual hunters would probably just throw in the towel and wait for better weather. But I had no choice. I had traveled all the way from Maine to Massachusetts, and only had three days to hunt. Besides, I was prepared.

The next morning I piled on every piece of warm clothing I had brought, then topped it off with a layer of rain gear. From a quick scouting trip the day before, I determined the best location to set up would be against a stone wall that separated two fields. Unfortunately, without a canopy of trees to protect me, the soaking rain managed to seep into every chink in my Gore-Tex armor, and after an hour of sitting in the steady rain, both my spirits and my body were thoroughly dampened. My only consolation was that the wind had abated, somewhat.

I peered from under my hood, like Charlie Sheen in the movie *Platoon*, continually scanning slowly from side to side for any sign of "the enemy." About the eleven-hundredth scan, I caught site of something moving down the corn stubble toward me—turkeys! Ever so slowly, I eased my body around to a semi-prone position on the wall. I had a solid rest for my gun, and the birds were headed straight to me. All I had to do was wait.

I hadn't realized just how cold I was until the sudden rush of adrenaline warmed me up a little. I tried to keep from shaking as the birds slowly closed the distance. Picking away at waste corn they came—100 yards, 75, 50. At 30 yards distance, a big tom stopped and his head suddenly jerked up. He was staring directly at me but it was too late; my bead was on him. The first shot rolled the bird, but he got up and made a wide loop, circling back within range again. The second shot planted him.

Several factors contributed to that success, but one of the most important was having the right clothing. A good many unequipped hunters probably would have passed on a day like that, and a fair number of ill-equipped ones probably wouldn't have lasted long in the cold, driving rain. Being comfortable allowed me to stay long enough to fill

So-called snake boots provide the best all-around footwear for the spring turkey hunter, offering a durable exterior, good ankle support and rugged sole for rough terrain. Waterproof models round out your footwear needs.

my tag. Since then I've had many more successes, a fair number of which were partly due to having the right clothing for a variety of conditions. What follows is a run-down of necessities and suggestions for turkey hunting apparel.

FOOTWEAR

Let's start from the bottom and work up. Obviously, you'll need a pair of boots. Your two primary concerns should be comfort and concealment. While camouflage boots are not necessary, they're worthy of strong consideration. Anything that helps you to better blend into your surroundings is an asset. At the very least, you need a pair of dark-colored boots with no shiny buckles, clips or grommets. Sunlight reflecting off anything shiny could be enough to give away your presence.

How much support you need in a boot will vary, depending on how and where you hunt. If you spend most of your time hunting the farm field edges of southern New England, you can get by with less. If you do a lot of walking, particularly in mountainous areas like Vermont and New Hampshire, you'll need a boot with plenty of ankle and arch support, and a good, rugged tread.

Moisture is also a strong consideration. I annually hunt four or five of the six New England states and some years it seems to rain wherever I go. Even when it doesn't, vegetation is often soaked with dew first thing in the morning. Also, your travels may take you through swampy areas or across streams. You can go a long way toward keeping your feet dry with either knee-high rubber boots or leather boots lined with a waterproofing material like Gore-Tex. For years I exclusively wore LaCrosse Burlys, and still do on rainy days. On drier days, or when hunting more mountainous areas, I now wear knee-high "snake boots," lined with Gore-Tex. The lace-up design provides more support and a tighter fit, which means less slippage and fewer blisters. I'm not worried about snakes, but the leather and Cordura nylon uppers hold up better than rubber against abrasion and sharp objects. This style boot also breathes better than a rubber boot.

Footwear also includes socks. Remember the motto: Cotton is rotten. Cotton absorbs and retains moisture, leaving you with cold, wet feet, which will blister more easily. A better choice is a thin polypropylene or acrylic sock liner with a Thermax, wool or wool-blend sock, lighter when it's warm, and heavier when it's cool. Combining this system with a Gore-Tex boot will wick moisture away from your feet, keeping them dry and comfortable.

OUTERWEAR & UNDERWEAR

You have a lot of leeway in terms of what you wear for pants and shirt, with one notable exception: They must be camouflaged. Cotton is fine, particularly when temperatures are warm, as it will retain moisture and cool you off. In cool or rainy weather, wool or synthetics are better, as they wick moisture away from your body, and continue to insulate when wet. One of the best fabrics I've come across is

Turkeys are still out there when it rains, and you should be, too.

Microsuede, treated with Repelzz. Microsuede combines the durable comfort of cotton with the moisture-wicking properties of polypropylene, and when treated with Repelzz, sheds water like a duck's back.

Another consideration, particularly with regard to pants, is durability. Turkeys seem to favor areas with lots of thorns and barbed wire, and you'll need something that is tear-resistant and tough. That's why denim is better than plain cotton. Some pants also come with double-layered legs and knees. They may seem a bit extravagant, until the first time you get hung up in a briar patch.

What you wear over and under your pants and shirt will depend on several things, including weather and temperature. The key is to dress in layers, and err on the side of too much clothing. You can always remove layers, but you can't add them if you don't have them with you.

More often than not, early to mid-May mornings in New England start out cold, with temperatures sometimes close to the freezing mark. Most mornings, the first layer I put on consists of polypropylene or Thermax underwear. It breathes well and wicks away perspiration, while providing an extra layer of insulation. Over this, I wear my standard shirt and pants. If it's cool, I may add a fleece sweatshirt. I prefer fleece for its nonabsorbent, insulating qualities. If it's really cold, I may

Three-dimensional suits offer an added dimension to your camouflage outerwear.

opt for a Thinsulate-lined coat, and it's added insulation. Rain offers the additional challenge of trying to stay dry. In a light drizzle you may simply opt for fleece or Microsuede. A heavier rain requires Gore-Tex jacket or parka and pants. In fact, I know some hunters who wear Gore-Tex pants on sunny days to protect against heavy dew, and ground moisture when sitting. In addition to not having to worry about scent, the turkey hunter can also be less concerned than the deer hunter about noise. You can get away with rain gear that is a bit more noisy than your deer hunting garb. Still, the quieter the better. In any case, camo is again essential. A hooded parka is okay during a heavy rain, but I find the hood restricts my peripheral vision. Forget about cheap vinyl rain gear. After one day afield it will end up looking more like a ghillie suit.

Speaking of ghillie suits, they are a great accessory. One minor drawback with conventional camo clothing is that it is two-dimensional. Turkeys may only have binocular vision when looking straight ahead, but the better you blend into your surroundings, the less chance you have of being detected. Military snipers figured this out long ago, and the hunting fraternity has more recently caught on. Several companies market three-dimensional "leafy wear," and I can say from personal experience that the stuff works. A less expensive but more labor-intensive option is pin-on leaves, marketed under trade names like Sneaky Leaf and Cover System. You may look kind of silly to your fellow turkey hunters, but it is you who will have the last laugh when you stroll into camp with a big gobbler over your shoulder.

HEADWEAR

You have several options to choose from regarding hats. Obviously, camouflage is a requirement. A visor is helpful to shade your eyes from the sun. However, a full brim can block sound. That's why I prefer a baseball cap style. A mesh back is better for warm conditions and solid back for cooler days. A camo wool or fleece cap offers more comfort on cold mornings and, of course, wear Gore-Tex on rainy days.

OTHER

A couple of other accessories you'll need are a head-net and gloves. Both should be camo or drab in color. I usually lose a couple pairs of gloves over the course of the season so I keep a good supply on hand, and always carry at least one extra pair afield. Cotton gloves are fine, and if you want to save money you can pick up brown Jersey gloves at most hardware stores for a few dollars a pair. The type of headnet you use will depend largely on personal preference. I prefer a cooler, ventilated mesh material over solid cotton. I also prefer a three-quarter mask rather than a full hood, as I can pull it down and wear it loosely around my neck when I'm not working a bird. Lastly, I prefer a mask with a wire rim around the eyes. This allows me to shape the mask opening tight to my eyes, whereas more loose-fitting masks will sometimes obscure my peripheral vision.

BEATING THE BUGS

I killed my first gobbler on a warm morning in May. The bird was responding well to my calls, so I settled in against the bole of a big oak, propped my gun up and waited. As turkeys often do, he stopped about 50 yards out and went into strut, closing the remaining distance at a painstakingly slow pace. I couldn't see him, but I could hear his soft footfalls on the dry leaves, and the occasional spit and drum. This only enhanced my already excited state, and my heavy breathing filled the air with carbon dioxide, serving as a beacon for every mosquito within a

Try to match your camo pattern to the habitat and time of the season you'll be hunting. Darker colors with more brown and gray are better for early-season, while those with more green are better later in the spring. The reverse is true in the fall.

hundred yards. They pierced the skin of my nose, ears and around my eyes, but I dared not move, for fear of spooking the gobbler. Those moments of anguish were forgotten once I pulled the trigger, but at the time they seemed almost unbearable.

One of the major nuisances of turkey hunting is bugs. In addition to May flowers, April showers also bring black flies and mosquitoes. Fortunately, the turkey's sense of smell is not well-developed, and we can spray ourselves down with insect repellent without fear of being detected. Of course, repellent only lasts so long, and unless you carry it with you in the field, its effects will soon wear off. Incidentally, recent studies have clearly demonstrated that DEET repellents are the most effective and long-lasting, and are not harmful to humans.

As an alternative, you can wear a full, bug-proof mesh suit. A mosquito's stinger can easily penetrate most light cotton garments but not the mesh. Many also come with head-net and gloves. When the bugs are particularly bad, I sometimes wear a bug suit, but have found the net obscured my vision too much; so I still cover my face with repellent.

Perhaps less of a nuisance but a much greater threat to human health are ticks. Wood ticks can carry rocky mountain spotted fever and deer ticks are known vectors of Lyme disease, human granulocytic ehrlichiosis and babesiosis, all of which can be contracted by humans. Standard insect repellents with DEET will work against them, but better tick repellents contain Duralon or Permethrin. These are designed to be sprayed not on the body but on your clothing, and will remain effective for several weeks. During a recent turkey season, I treated my turkey clothing with a product called No Stinkin' Ticks, hunted in seven states, including Connecticut, and never had a single tick or chigger on me. Another way to beat ticks is with Rynoskin undergarments. This tight-fitting synthetic material provides a tick-proof barrier between your skin and outer clothing without overheating you.

CAMO PATTERNS

When it comes to camo patterns, today's turkey hunters have so many choices they may find it difficult (if not impossible) to pick one. Really, it's not that tough. The general goal of camouflage is to disguise the wearer by creating contrast, and breaking up the outline of the human form. Because turkeys can distinguish colors quite well, color accuracy is also important. For these reasons, most camo patterns consist predominantly of various shades of gray, green and brown, which offer both accurate color and proper tonal range.

General purpose patterns like Mossy Oak Break-Up, Reeltree Hardwoods and Advantage Timber are designed to work in a variety of habitats. The dark and light gray matrix, designed to simulate a tree trunk, disguises you well against the trunk of a tree. Conversely, the greens will help you blend in against ground cover and leafy saplings.

Meanwhile, lighter browns simulate the effect of mottled sunlight filtering through the canopy onto the forest floor.

Most New England turkey seasons span much or all of the month of May. From start to finish, the woods can change considerably, from the bleak grays and browns of early May to the lush greens of late May. General purpose patterns will work throughout, but you may want to have several different outfits to adapt to the changing environment. For example, the brownish dead-leaf patterns of Advantage Classic and Mossy Oak Forest Floor blend in well early in the season, before leaf-out. Later, you may want to switch to something like Hardwoods Green, Advantage Timber or Mossy Oak Shadow Leaf. Some hunters will actually mix and match patterns, wearing darker pants with more browns and grays, and shirts with more green. In my opinion the best, all-around spring pattern is Realtree Xtra Brown. Alas, they don't make it anymore. If you can't afford to be a camo connoisseur, don't despair. Good old fashioned three-color military surplus camo will do just fine.

As you can see, clothing is a key ingredient in the recipe for turkey hunting success. You need something that will keep you dry when it's wet, warm when it's cold, will protect you against thorns and bugs and will conceal you from the turkey's keen vision. The more comfortable you are and the more functional your clothing, the better, longer and harder you'll hunt. And your hunt will be more enjoyable.

six

GUNS & AMMO

six

It was the evening before the Bay State's 1999 turkey opener, and I was headed to a likely spot to try to roost a bird. As I motored up to the cornfield, I was greeted with more than I could have hoped for. There stood a dozen birds, including four big toms. One had a beard of at least eleven inches, another, a beard as broad and thick as a paintbrush. "A real trophy," I thought. I watched the birds hop a stone wall and disappear into the woodlot just at dark. No owl calling would be necessary. The following morning I had my decoys out and was in position well before daylight. The woods were remarkably silent as the sun started its slow ascent, and I began to wonder what had gone wrong. Shortly after sunup, however, a hen launched from her roost, lit on the ground nearby, then sauntered by, mere feet from me. I watched her out of the corner of my eye as she hopped the wall and wandered out into the cornfield. Soon, another hen followed the same route. My heart was racing, for I knew the gobblers should be close behind. But they weren't.

Long minutes passed with no more turkeys. My confidence waned over the next hour, and I stayed put another hour, more out of a lack of options than any hope the birds would show. As it turned out, I was wrong again.

Scarce moments later I caught a movement to my left. Ever so slowly I turned to see four red heads bobbing their way toward me along the stone wall. It was the toms! When all four disappeared behind a big pine, I eased my gun around to the left and into shooting position. I could hear the birds scratching their way along, moving closer with each step. I expected at any moment they would reappear from behind the tree, at what should be chip-shot distance. The noise continued, but still no sign of the birds. Then I saw them. They had turned behind the tree and were now moving down and away, on the other side of a draw, over thirty yards distance, and increasing the gap with each step. My excitement was turning to desperation. The opportunity was quickly disappearing when, at forty-plus yards, the last bird paused just long enough to offer a clear shot.

Under ordinary circumstances, I might not take a shot at that distance. However, I was testing Federal's High Energy 3 1/2-inch loads, and Mossberg's 835 Ulti-Mag shotgun, and this provided an ideal opportunity. I knew forty yards was well within my effective range as I'd patterned the loads and gun out to fifty yards. The Mossberg roared. The gobbler dropped on the spot and never so much as twitched. When I finally made it to the bird and turned him over, I saw it was the bird with the paintbrush beard.

That success was attributable to several things. First, I had a combination of gun and ammunition designed specifically for turkey hunting. Second, I knew the capabilities of my firearm and ammunition. Patience and luck also played a big part, as they often do in turkey hunting. If you're the lucky type, you can entrust your chances of success to the vagaries of fate. But if you can select equipment that will boost your chances of success, doesn't it make sense to do so? One way you can do that is with your choice of guns and ammunition. What follows is a rundown of options, and some advice on what the best choices might be.

FIREARMS

Most veteran New England turkey hunters probably took their first birds with their favorite fowling piece or upland bird gun, because that's all that was available for turkey hunting when they started. Today's turkey hunters have a lot more options, including guns specifically designed for the sport. While you can kill a turkey with just about any shotgun, if you're going to get serious about turkey hunting, you may want to consider buying or building a gun specifically for that purpose. Certain types have some significant advantages.

GAUGE

Let's begin with bore. Unless you plan on limiting your shots to under twenty yards, you should consider nothing less than a 12 gauge. You may only get one chance, and you don't want to risk missing or wounding a bird. A 10 gauge will offer a slight advantage in terms of effective range and knockdown power, but you'll pay for it in addition-

Some of the author's favorite turkey guns (l. to r.): Mossberg Model 9200, Remington 870 Express, Mossberg 870 Ulti-Mag, Mossberg 500 and Knight TK2000.

al recoil. A good friend of mine hunts exclusively with his trusty old Ithaca Mag 10, which he affectionately refers to as "Maggie." He's killed over 100 birds with it, but I've noticed when he walks, his left shoulder is always a little farther ahead of his right. A 20 gauge might be a better option for younger hunters, women or small-framed men. However, you'll have to let the bird get a bit closer than you would with larger-bored guns.

ACTION

The type of action you choose depends, to a great extent on personal preference. With regard to not only action, but all aspects, you should choose the gun you are most comfortable with. Still, certain types offer certain advantages. Probably the greatest advantage of the break-action, single-shot is simplicity. It's easy to use, and there aren't a lot of moving parts to jam up. Side-by-side and over-and-under guns offer the same simplicity, with the added bonus of a second shot, which can sometimes come in handy. All have some shortcomings.

The major drawback of the single-shot is lack of a quick follow-up, if needed. One drawback of side-by-sides is consistent accuracy between barrels. Doubles are designed for wingshooting, where you point and shoot, spraying a pattern of shot at a moving target. The turkey hunter must aim and shoot at a more or less stationery target, which requires accuracy.

When selecting a shotgun, the most important consideration is finding a gun that you are comfortable with and can shoot well.

Another drawback, also common to the over-and-unders, is overall accuracy. In most cases you're relying on a single bead sight, and again, shotguns are generally designed to spread shot over a large area to cover a moving target, not to hit a single, specific point.

Slide-actions or semi-autos offer several distinct advantages. First, and perhaps foremost, is a follow-up shot. I've rolled several birds with my first shot, only to have them right themselves and start to run away. Were it not for a quick follow-up, I might have lost them. A second shot is also handy if you have multiple tags in your pocket. As cagey as turkeys are, they sometimes react very peculiarly to the sound of a shotgun and their running mate suddenly flopping on the ground. It's not at all uncommon for other birds to freeze at the shot, and I've even had toms come over and begin spurring a bird I'd just shot.

Perhaps the greatest advantage to pumps and autoloaders is that this is where most of the more recent innovations in turkey guns have been applied. Firearms manufacturers have responded to the relatively recent, dramatic increase in the popularity of turkey hunting by producing shotguns designed specifically for the sport. Most of the larger companies now offer turkey guns in both pump and semi-automatic.

The downside to guns with moving parts is they are prone to the occasional jam. But that is so rare in modern shotguns that it should be of little concern.

CHOKE

Perhaps just as important as gauge is choke. For the most part, turkey hunters use lead shot, and the general rule-of-thumb with choke is: the tighter, the better. You want to deliver as many pellets as possible to your target, and tighter chokes can increase your effective range. Full is the best choice for a fixed-choke gun. Most newer shotguns come equipped to handle interchangeable chokes. This is a handy alternative if you only own one shotgun and plan to use it for other game. Virtually all of the major gun makers also make "super-full" or turkey chokes, and many other companies offer after-market chokes that will fit most of the major brands of guns. In some cases, after-market chokes offer even tighter constrictions, allowing you to "fine-tune your choke-shot load combination.

More recently, some ammo manufacturers have introduced nontoxic shot loads for turkey hunting. Remington's Hevi-shot is an example. Originally designed as a nontoxic alternative for waterfowling, this shot type has been shown to hold remarkably dense patterns. However, because it is much harder than lead and does not deform, a more open choke is recommended.

CHAMBER

The other major option in shotguns is chamber length. Hunters have been killing turkeys long before anyone ever got around to designing loads specifically for that purpose. However, now that ammo manufacturers are doing so, there's no reason not to take advantage of it. The

Turkey hunters can choose from a variety of sights for their guns. Shown here (l. to r.) are: BSA Red-dot, Bushnell 4x scope, Bushnell Holo-sight and Tru-Glo fiber-optic sights.

three-inch chamber was originally designed with the waterfowler in mind, but turkey hunters were quick to take advantage of the superior ballistics. Most new shotguns come with a 3-inch chamber, and it was pretty much the standard among turkey guns, for a while. Like its predecessor, the 3½-inch chamber was intended originally for waterfowlers—a response to the mandatory change to steel shot. When filled with lead however, the 3½-inch shell provides a premium 12-gauge turkey load that rivals the ten-gauge, with considerably less punishment to the shooter.

The major, and perhaps only, disadvantage of moving up in chamber size is the additional recoil. But under hunting conditions, you rarely notice it. Incidentally, recoil absorption is another advantage of the pump-action or semi-auto actions.

Remington, Federal and Winchester incorporate buffered, copper-plated lead shot into their turkey loads. The copper plating makes the shot harder, so there is less deformation in the barrel, and thus fewer flyers. With the shot, they add a synthetic buffering material, causing the shot to hold a tighter pattern.

SIGHTS

Turkey hunters also have a variety of sight types to choose from. The basic single-bead sight found on most general-purpose shotguns is acceptable, but has its limitations. Most notably, it only gives you one point of aim. The number one reason for missed turkeys (at least those that are in range) is hunters lifting their cheek off the stock to peek over the barrel. The bead may still be on the bird but the gun is actually aimed over the bird's head. Two beads, front and back, are better, but sometimes hard to distinguish in low light.

Most turkey guns now come standard with fiber optic rifle sights in various configurations. The most common is a single bead in the front and two in the rear, side-by-side with a small space between, so you can line up all three like a rifle sight. Having two points of aim helps keep your cheek on the stock and the fiber optics glow in low light, making them easier to see. If your favorite turkey gun doesn't have them, you can buy after-market types that can be affixed to most any type of shotgun. There are also several types of more complicated sighting devices that can be affixed to your barrel or receiver. Some clip on to the vent rib, some are magnetic, and others can be affixed to the receiver, if it is drilled and tapped, or attached to a saddle mount, over the receiver.

An even better choice for some people are optical sights, and the options are many and varied. A shotgun scope offers magnification and a reticle for greater accuracy. Any type will do, but some now come with reticles designed specifically for turkey hunting. In any case, anything in the 2x to 4x power range will suffice if you desire magnification. Rather than a wire reticle, some come with an illuminated red dot, or holographic reticle in the center of the scope. Most of these lack magnification, but at 30 yards you don't really need it.

FINISH

Though not as important as how well it shoots, how your gun looks is also worthy of consideration. Most modern turkey guns come in camouflage, and you may have several choices of the latest designer patterns. Is it necessary? No, but it helps, and it sure looks good. The truth is, the more camouflaged you and your hunting equipment are, the less chance you'll be noticed. Camouflage is best, but you can get by with a black synthetic or unpolished, brown wooden stock, and a plain, matte-finish barrel. If you plan to turkey hunt with a gun that has a polished, blued barrel and receiver, and a bowling-ball-finished stock, you'll need to camouflage it. You can do this with a gun sock, no-mar tape or a can of spray paint. Don't laugh. My first turkey gun was a shiny, new Mossberg Model 500. When I got it home, I took out three cans of removable, camo spray paint and went to work. You don't need removable paint, but it comes off easily by spraying the gun down with paint remover.

Vital Areas in the Head of a Wild Turkey

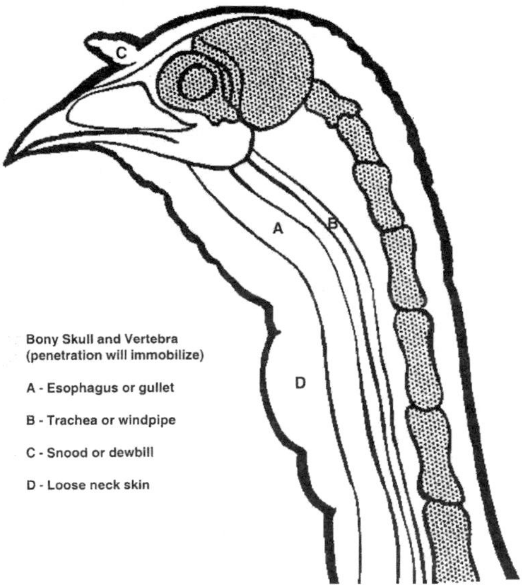

Make photocopies for patterning your gun.

REPRINTED BY PERMISSION OF MAINE DEPARTMENT OF INLAND FISHERIES & WILDLIFE.

AMMUNITION

Shot Size

If you put 12 veteran turkey hunters in a room, and asked each what the optimum shot size for turkey hunting is, I'd venture to guess you'd get at least four, maybe more, different answers. Conventional wisdom says that sizes 4, 5 and 6 are among the best. Still, I know some hunters that use 2s and others that swear by $7^{1/2}$s. My response is: Use whatever works best for you. Still, you can't go wrong by sticking somewhere in the middle. I've used 4, 5 and 6, and experienced favorable results with each in the field. The difference becomes more pronounced on the range, which I'll discuss more in the next section. Most (ethical) shots at turkeys are within 30 yards, where 4 and 6 shot have similar energy and knockdown power. Then, the edge goes to the smaller shot size because it offers more pellets. If you still can't decide, Remington sells "duplex" loads that contain both 4 and 6 shot.

Shot Pattern or Arrow Placement for a Quick Kill

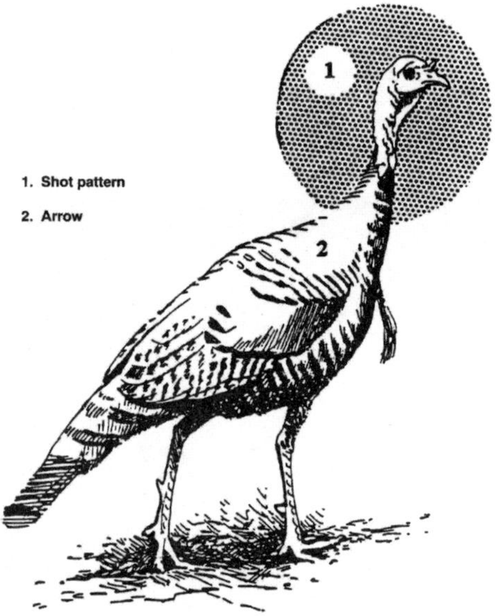

REPRINTED BY PERMISSION OF MAINE DEPARTMENT OF INLAND FISHERIES & WILDLIFE.

Shot Type

Until fairly recently, the only real choice for turkey shot was lead. It's still the most common and popular type, though there are several variations and alternatives. Plain old lead shot will work just fine. However, many ammo companies are now marketing loads specifically for turkey hunting. Those from the big three, Remington, Federal and Winchester, incorporate buffered, copper-plated lead shot into their turkey loads. The copper plating makes the shot harder, so there is less deformation in the barrel and fewer flyers. With the shot, they add a synthetic buffering material, which makes the shot hold a tighter pattern. As mentioned, Remington also sells Hevi-shot, a non-toxic alloy that has a similar density to lead, and holds extremely tight patterns. It should be noted that lead shot may not be legal on some federal lands.

Loads

Bigger is better; it's the American way. While standard loads will kill a turkey, magnum loads will do it better. The big three ammo manufacturers all sell magnum or high velocity turkey loads. They provide more shot to increase pellet count, and more powder to compensate for the heavier loads.

Patterning

Regardless of what gauge, action, chamber or shot size you select, the most critical part of optimizing your turkey gun is patterning. You *must* pattern your gun before you hunt. I own a Mossberg 9200, semi-auto that I acquired specifically for turkey hunting. It came equipped with Tru-Glo sights and a super-full turkey choke. Out of the box it shot an exceptionally tight pattern, but hit consistently high and left. Had I not taken the time to pattern it, it could easily have cost me a bird. By adding adjustable sights, I was able to "tune it in."

That's an extreme example, but those who are willing to devote the time and expense necessary are often astounded by the results. Every gun shoots a little differently. Furthermore, different guns shoot different brands of ammo and different shot sizes differently, and performance can vary considerably with different chokes, guns and ammo. In some cases, standard 2¾-inch loads may actually pattern better than three-inch loads in your gun, and harder, copper-plated shot may pattern better in a full or modified choke than in a super-full turkey choke. You may find your gun patterns better with Winchester, Remington, or Federal ammunition. The only way to find out is to practice before you hunt.

MUZZLELOADERS

Modern shotguns aren't the only firearms with which you can hunt turkeys in New England. Some traditionalists, and those seeking an added challenge, have taken up muzzleloading shotguns in their pursuit of the elusive turkey. Available models range from authentic antiques to modern versions with in-line ignition systems. Most come with simple bead sights, though newer ones and in-lines typically have fiber-optic sights.

Rather than an enclosed shotshell, the components of your loads include powder, shot, shotcup wad and overshot wad. For powder, you may use black powder or any of its modern substitutes. Never use

Advancements in modern muzzleloaders have prompted many turkey hunters to take up the added challenge of hunting with a smokepole.

smokeless powder. Your owner's manual should have recommended powder charge sizes. If not, you should be using something in the neighborhood of 90 to 100 grains. Also, pellets are not recommended for shotguns; stick to loose powder. For shot, use chilled lead shot, available wherever shotgun reloading supplies are found. You can use standard shotgun wads, but those designed for muzzleloaders will hold twice the amount of shot used in a standard 2¾-inch shotshell. Finally, the overshot wad will hold the shot in place.

You have several choices in ignition systems. Flintlocks are not available on most newer guns, and prone to misfire. Still, they may be preferred by the blackpowder purist. Most modern muzzleloading shotguns are equipped with a caplock ignition system, including side-hammer and inline types. Some of the newer in-lines are ignited by a 209 shotgun primer. The latter is the most reliable type, as it seals the nipple, preventing any moisture from reaching the powder.

Along with shot components, you'll need the usual possibles: a nipple or breech-plug wrench and nipple pick for in-the-field cleaning between shots, or in the event of a misfire. You can speed up your reloading time by carrying pre-measured powder and shot charges in air-tight "speed-loader" capsules, and by using a capping tool, preloaded with caps.

Patterning your muzzleloader is more important and involved, but offers several advantages. First, you're not restricted by fixed loads. Because you can vary both shot and powder in small increments, you can tinker until you find just the right combination. Also, because you can buy both in bulk, patterning is less expensive.

Though it may seem rather complex, choosing the right shotgun (or muzzleloader) and loads for turkey hunting is not that difficult. With what you've just learned you can now make an informed choice, and most reputable sporting goods retailers should have enough options to fit your needs. Once you have a gun, you'll then need to acquire a few other odds and ends to fill out your turkey hunting regalia.

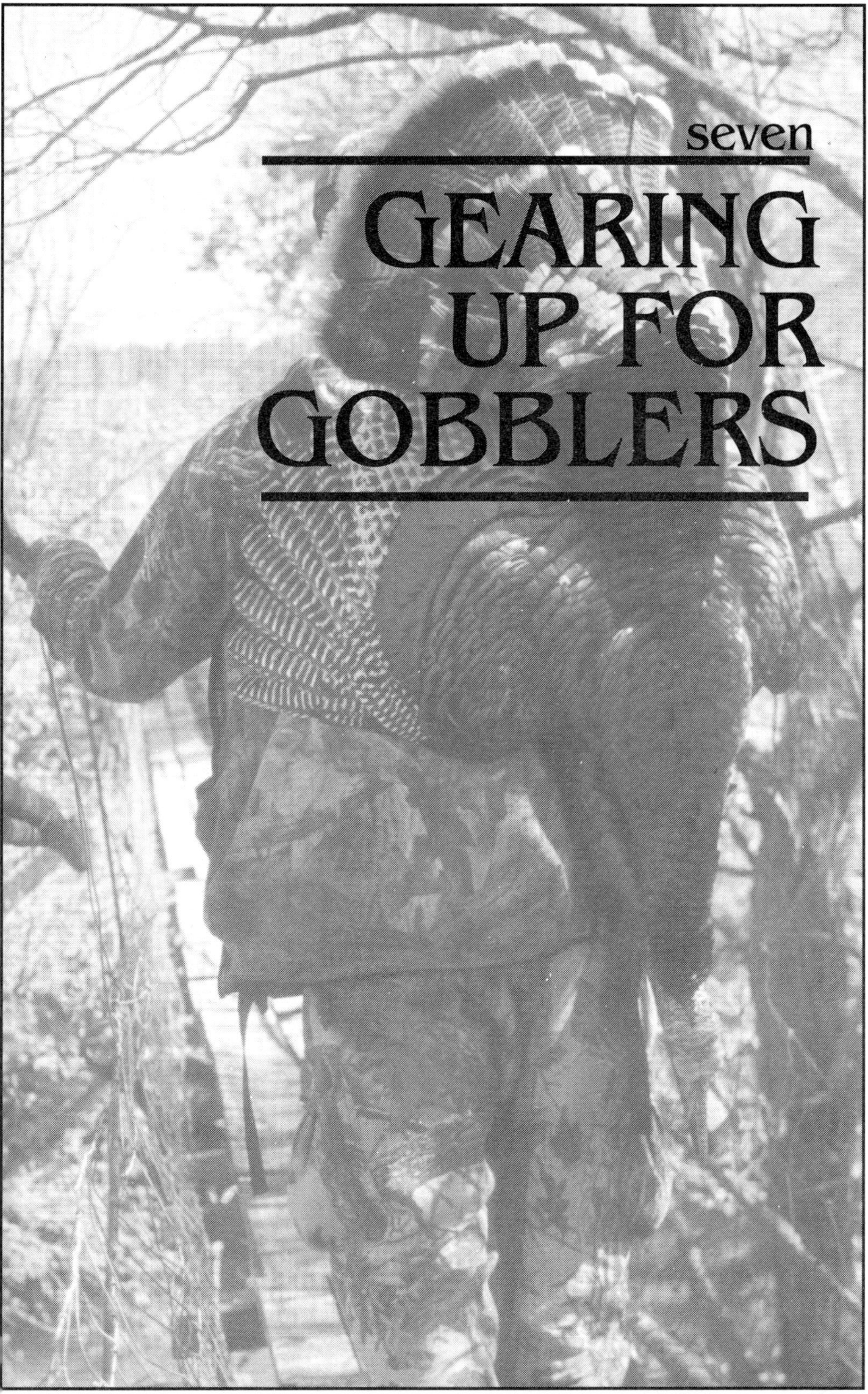

seven

GEARING UP FOR GOBBLERS

seven

Our meager breakfast done, George Mayfield and I prepared our gear for a morning of turkey hunting in the Green Mountains of Vermont. Actually, I was doing most of the preparing, while George stood by the door waiting patiently. As we stepped out into the moonlight, we looked about as different as two turkey hunters could. A single striker protruded from George's breast pocket, which also showed the ringed impression of the solitary slate call it contained. Around his neck hung a small pouch containing several of his favorite mouth calls. He stuffed a handful of shells in his pants pocket, hefted his gun and had all he needed. I, on the other hand, was weighed down with a heavy vest, and all of the various and sundry items it contained.

His sparse equipment list suited George's run-and-gun hunting style. He likes to move fast and far, finding the birds wherever they are. This being his first day in camp, he also planned to spend a considerable amount of it scouting and familiarizing himself with the territory. I, on the other hand, prefer the more traditional approach: roosting birds, setting up on them and calling them to me. I also had the advantage of being familiar with the area, and hadn't really planned on covering much ground. I'd intended to set up in a known location and wait the birds out. And for that style of hunting, I felt everything I carried was quite necessary. Later, though, as I set out my decoys and settled in against the bole of a big pine, I began to ponder the differences in the amount and type of gear we each carried afield.

Truth be known, there's almost no limit to the stuff we hunters can carry afield with us. But if you wanted to bring along one of everything, you'd need a Sherpa to carry it all. Much of what's available could be considered optional accessories, or even luxuries. Yet a good deal of it can, under various circumstance, be quite necessary. Deciding which is which can also vary from person to person, and day to day. You may be

While not everything you carry with you may be necessary, the more "stuff" you tote, the more options you'll have. Pictured here are all of the items I carry afield with me.

able to get by with just a few items for a quick morning hunt. If you're planning on spending the day in the woods however, or there's a chance of rain, you'll almost certainly need more and different equipment. The following are some suggestions of what I consider the more essential items your turkey vest should contain, with some options for various circumstances and conditions. As you spend more time afield, you can add or subtract from the list to suit your individual needs and hunting style.

CALLS

I recall an opening morning several years ago when, as is often the case in turkey hunting, things didn't go quite as planned. I'd roosted a bird the night before and set up on him well before daylight. My decoys were out, and I greeted the dawn's early light with a soft serenade of tree calls, later followed by a fly-down cackle and some full-blown yelping. When the old tom bailed out however, he had other ideas. He hit the ground and began gobbling at my every call, as he headed away in the opposite direction. The bird disappeared into the woods and had barely gone out of hearing when a shotgun blast ended his gobbling, and my morning plan.

The sun still hadn't crested the treetops, and I knew there were other birds around, so I moved down the hill, reset my decoys and laid out my calls. I started with a few loud yelps on a box, but got no response. I switched immediately to a slate, getting the same results. Then, I popped in a diaphragm, and before I could finish my bout, I was answered with a very close gobble. My next attempt was cut short as well, and I'd scarcely settled my shotgun on my knee when a resplendent red, white and blue head and a fanned tail materialized over the rise.

I always carry a variety of calls, and that morning reminded me of why. Gobblers can, on occasion, be very finicky. Different birds respond to different calls, and the same bird may react differently on different days. Sometimes you have to do a little experimenting to find the call that appeals to a particular bird on a particular day, and the more options you have, the better the odds you'll be able to strike the right cord.

Variety is particularly important if you travel to hunt, as I learned during a recent spring. I was hunting in Texas, and the calls I'd used two weeks earlier in South Carolina's low country just didn't seem to suit the local birds. It took a little experimenting, but I soon found the birds responded much better to higher-pitched calls. Comparing notes later with one of my companions, I learned he'd discovered the same thing, and our luck soon changed.

For those reasons, I always carry multiple calls, usually two box calls, two slates and a half-dozen diaphragms with me on every outing. The key is to pick calls with very different tones. I'll cover the topic of calls in much more detail in the next chapter.

DECOYS

Though it wasn't always the case, I rarely hunt without decoys now. One of the leading causes of birds hanging up out of range is toms that come to the call expecting to see a hen, but don't. If nothing else, a hen decoy adds confidence to your calling. It also gives the tom something else to focus his attention on besides you when he's in the "red zone."

Decoy manufacturers have addressed the issue of portability by making decoys light, collapsible and easier to transport in your vest. Three decoys and their stakes weigh only a few ounces, and will fit neatly into

Decoys offer many advantages. How and when you use them and how many you use will vary according to each situation.

the game pouch on most vests. Motion in your decoys can also be key, so I prefer the type that can spin on their stake with the wind. Incidentally, it doesn't hurt to carry an extra stake or two in case you lose or break one, and I usually carry a screwdriver to jab starter holes in hard ground.

MISCELLANEOUS

There's almost no limit to the number and variety of other items you can take with you into the woods, but there are several that, like the above items, should be considered necessities.

First, and perhaps foremost, is a "call-care" kit. Most friction calls require some maintenance as you use them. You'll need chalk for your box calls, and small patches of sandpaper and scrub pads for your slates. All of this will fit neatly into a snuff can, or even a film canister. Several companies make call tools, some about the size of a toothbrush, with faces of various abrasive material for roughing up your slates.

You'll need a flashlight to find your way in the dark. Pick a small one that works on two AA batteries, or even a pen light to conserve space and weight. I know some hunters who even go so far as to use lights with red or green lenses, believing the white light will spook birds. In my experience that hasn't been the case, but if you feel a colored lens is better, go for it.

Another essential item for finding your way around is a compass. Of all the items you take with you afield, a compass may just be the single most important one. Take a bearing on the road and your direction of travel before you head in. You may also want to take bearings throughout the day to keep track of where you're going and which is the quickest way out. If you should wound a bird, you can take a bearing on which way he went, as wounded turkeys will often travel in a straight line. A multipurpose tool is handy to fashion decoy stakes, dislodge jammed shells, trim brush, adjust box calls and more.

If you plan on being in the woods for any length of time, you should bring along a small water bottle. On warm, dry days you'll find it well worth carrying the extra weight and should you get lost, it could mean survival. A light snack will help reenergize you and stave off hunger. I usually throw a few bite-sized candy bars in my vest for that reason, though I often end up with some funky-looking junk in the bottom of my pockets by season's end. You may also have to tend to other bodily functions, and while you can always resort to leaves, a wad of toilet tissue in a Ziploc bag is a much more comfortable option.

Make no mistake about it: Statistics show that turkey hunting can be dangerous. Most of the places I hunt are also used by other hunters. For reasons of safety and consideration for those I share the woods with, I carry an orange vest. Once I've bagged my bird, I load it in my turkey vest, then don the orange vest over it. Most turkey vests now come with orange flags that can be stowed in zippered pockets until needed.

A couple more things you might want to consider are an extra face mask and pair of camo gloves. They take up almost no space and add little weight, yet could come in real handy. I have a tendency to lose things and these two items are at the top of my "missing items" list.

THE VEST

Last but not least is the vest itself. What and how much you carry will, to some extent, determine what is the right vest for you. Some are small and light, and have only a few pockets. Others are larger, with many pockets, for pack rats like myself. You'll very likely spend a good deal of time sitting, and the ground can be cold, wet and uncomfortable. That's why I recommend a vest with a padded seat attached. Some vests even come with rigid internal frames to help support your back, a real plus when good cover is scarce.

Because I carry so much stuff, I like a vest with many pockets. More, smaller pockets keep me from fumbling through a few larger pockets to find what I need. It's also important that the pockets can be fastened, either with zippers, buttons or velcro. I learned this the hard way, and some of my most cherished possessions still lie out there somewhere in the turkey woods.

You should also consider a vest with a waterproof game pouch. The pouch can be used to carry decoys into the field and harvested birds out. It's also a good place to put excess clothing as the day warms and you strip off layers. Waterproof also means blood-proof, so your hunting clothes won't become blood-stained from toting out your hard-won prize.

Today the market is flooded with all sorts of turkey hunting gadgets, most of which are quite useful, but many of which could be considered nonessential. By carefully selecting the right items to take into the woods, you can ensure you'll have what you need, and increase the odds you'll be carrying more weight on your way out.

eight

SCOUT NOW, SCORE LATER

eight

It was the opening day of Maine's turkey season. A nasty head cold had kept me up most of the night, so I was already awake when the alarm went off at 2:30. That was ridiculously early, but I knew I'd have to beat the competition if I wanted to have my intended destination, and the big gobbler I'd roosted the night before, to myself. All was well when I arrived, so I grabbed up my hunting gear and a sleeping bag and started off across a big field. My intention was to move in close to the roost and take a long nap before the sun came up. Unfortunately, I never made it.

I heard the sound of car doors back at the road, and the next thing I knew, I was standing in the beam of a one million-candle-power spotlight. I stood and stared in disbelief as I watched the beam bounce across the field in my direction. The two shadows behind the light stopped ten yards away and stood silently, leaving me to break the stand-off.

I bit my tongue and, as calmly as I could, inquired, "What are you doing?" The shadows cleared their throats, moved a bit closer, then mustered up enough gumption (even more than they'd already demonstrated), to explain that they too had planned on hunting this field. As they'd already tromped directly under the roost with their light, I figured my plans were busted anyway, so I yielded the field and left them to scare off anyone else who might arrive that morning.

Thanks to my preseason scouting efforts, I knew of another location, where I had been watching the morning routine of another gobbler. I jumped in my truck and raced across town, then bailed out and headed for the woods. I arrived a bit late, but with just enough time to sneak into position and set up. The treetops were ringing with gobbles from at least three directions of my location. The closest birds were to my right, so I focused my attention their way.

The more they gobbled in response to my calls, the more and the louder I called. When they flew down however, it soon became apparent they were going away from me. It was decision time. The most vocal birds were headed away, but I'd seen one tom where I now sat every morning for the past week. Should I stay or should I go?

I again decided to rely on my pre-season scouting, and stayed put. As the flock of gobblers faded out of hearing, I noticed another, single tom, still gobbling to my calls. He was on the far side of two large fields, which were divided by a road. It seemed a longshot, so I called as loudly as I could, and he answered every time. It took a while for him to cross the first field. When he came to the road, he bolted across and ran a full 300 yards up the second field, stopping at about 75 yards from me, where he puffed up into a full strut. Ever so slowly, he closed the final 50 yards, whereupon I squeezed the trigger, ending a very long early morning hunt.

With turkey hunting, as with deer hunting, the more time you spend scouting, the less time you'll spend hunting. Furthermore, the closer to hunting season you scout, the more useful the information you collect. The key is in knowing what to look for, and how to interpret what you find. If your time is limited, it's even more important. Otherwise, you could be wasting a lot of precious time.

Obviously, to begin you need to find an area that holds turkeys. This can be done several ways. A quick phone call to the local state biologist is one. Word of mouth is another; folks love to talk about turkey sightings. Especially helpful is anyone who travels a regular route. I've found my local mail carrier to be a great source for recent turkey sightings. Still, the best source is first-hand observation.

PRESEASON SCOUTING

You can begin by merely driving the roads in potential turkey country. Due to work schedules or personal preference, a lot of folks do this in the afternoon. I've found early to mid-morning is the best time, however. This is when birds are most visible, and this is the time of day you'll ultimately be hunting. This is also when birds are most vocal, so you don't necessarily have to see them to know where they are.

While I may do some preliminary scouting in late winter, I usually wait until the breeding season begins before I devote any serious effort. Remember, winter flocks are disbanding and re-locating throughout the early spring, and they could move a long way before the hunting season.

Driving roads and looking for birds is a good way to get started with your scouting. However, turkeys that are regularly visible from the roadside will usually attract crowds of hunters, so don't be afraid to get back into the woods.

A typical scouting mission should begin about a half-hour before sunrise. Drive the local roads, stopping every quarter to half-mile to get out and listen for gobbling. Oftentimes, you'll be able to pinpoint a bird from one spot. Turkeys don't always roost in the same location though, so it's to your advantage to do this on several mornings, increasing your frequency as hunting season draws nearer.

As an alternative, you can sometimes locate birds by "roosting" them at dusk. Just after flying up to roost, turkeys will often react to any loud noise by gobbling. This reaction is referred to as "shock-gobbling." Most hunters attempt to roost turkeys by imitating the calls of barred owls or coyotes. Toms don't always shock gobble, so silence doesn't necessarily mean they're not there. That's why I believe morning scouting is better, as the birds will be gobbling of their own accord.

Sometimes you may not be able to precisely locate a distant gobbler. Then, topo maps can be especially helpful for locating by triangulation. Once you've located a bird, draw a pencil line on the map from your position to where you think the gobbler is. Move to another location and do this again. Once you've done this from three different locations, the intersection of the three lines identifies the gobbler's location. Locating birds away from the road takes more effort, but offers a distinct advantage-—less competition. Birds that frequent open areas are usually famous with the locals, and you can almost bet there will be a crowd there on opening day.

Now that you know where the birds are at dawn, you need to determine where they'll go when they leave the roost. This point is particularly important. So often hunters will set up on a gobbler they've roosted, only to have the bird fly down and go in the opposite direction (see first paragraph in Chapter 7). Where you call is much more important than how you call, and we'll discuss this more in a later chapter.

SIGN

If you don't have the time or determination to get up every morning at the crack of dawn to scout, or if you want to supplement your knowledge, you can set out on foot to look for sign. You can do this any time of day, but the middle of the day is best because the birds are less active, and you're less likely to disturb them.

Once you've found a locale that holds birds, you can begin to narrow down your search. Knowing a little about what's going on out there can help. For instance, if your hunting area had a good acorn crop the previous fall, turkeys will often be back in the oaks in the spring, looking for remnant acorns. If, on the other hand, it was a poor acorn year, or there aren't a lot of oaks in your area, look for other mast trees like beech and hickory. Nuts are high-calorie food, and turkeys relish them.

It's easy enough to figure out if the birds have been feeding in an area. They travel along the forest floor scratching the ground and leaves to uncover food, often leaving triangular-shaped patches of bare ground. Turkeys are much less delicate feeders than deer, and they'll scratch up big patches of leaves. Large areas of turned over leaves may indicate a lot of birds, or regular use. Either way, it's a good sign.

If you're still not sure whether it's turkey or deer sign, look for droppings. Turkeys leave black and white droppings that look much the same as any bird dropping, except larger. As mentioned in a previous chapter, you can even differentiate sexes by droppings. Hens leave a dropping that roughly resembles a popped corn kernel. The droppings of males are more linear, and often "J"-shaped.

In New England, I've observed that turkeys often go through a gradual transition in their spring diet. Essentially, they follow the green-up.

Signs for Locating Wild Turkeys

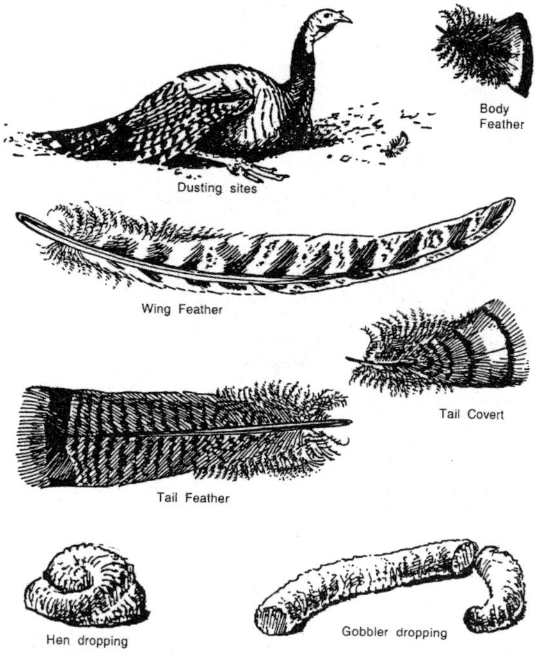

REPRINTED BY PERMISSION OF MAINE DEPARTMENT OF INLAND FISHERIES & WILDLIFE.

They'll usually begin feeding in river or stream bottoms, seeps or wetland areas, where the first green shoots come up. Here, they'll often find one of their preferred spring foods: skunk cabbage. Another popular early-spring food in the Northeast is Canada mayflower, or wild lily-of-the-valley, which grows in forested uplands. Again, look for scratchings.

Feeding is not the only activity that leaves evidence of turkey use. Every evening, turkeys fly to roost in large trees, often routinely using the same grove, or even the same trees. As they sit and preen, they'll drop feathers and poop. An accumulation of either, or both, is a good indication you've located a roost. Turkeys tend to prefer roosting in softwoods, when available, and you may also find a lot of small broken twigs on the ground under a roost.

You can also look for signs of courtship activity. A tom attracts a prospective mate first by gobbling. Once she is within sight he will puff up his feathers, fan his tail, droop his wings, and strut. Gobblers seem to prefer more open areas, such as fields, to strut in, but will also strut

When strutting, a gobbler will drag his wingtips on the ground. If you find drag marks, it is a good indication of a strut zone, and a good place to set up.

in forest openings, and along woods roads as well. They also frequently return to traditional strutting areas. If you find such a clearing in the woods, look for sign such as droppings and scratchings. If there is any exposed soil, you may also be able to make out strut marks made by the gobbler as he dragged his wingtips on the ground.

Another type of turkey sign, and one that is often overlooked, is a dusting site. This is little more than a concave bowl of exposed soil. It is formed when turkeys "bathe" in the dusty soil, presumably to rid themselves of parasites like feather lice. These bowls are somewhat analogous to deer scrapes. Although used for bathing rather than courtship, they are visited regularly, and can be especially productive later in the morning, after turkeys are done feeding.

This information is merely a primer to get you started in locating your gobbler. There's no substitute for experience, and the more time you spend afield in pursuit of turkeys, the more proficient you'll become. You need to be a good observer in the woods. Move slowly, and look for subtle evidence of turkey activity. If you have the opportunity, watch turkeys in the wild. Observe how they feed, what they eat, and when and where they travel. Before long, even the most obscure signs will jump out at you.

Turkeys frequently take dust baths to rid their feathers and body of parasites. They usually do this after they've finished their morning feeding routine. If you locate a dusting bowl, this might be a good place to set up later in the morning.

RECORD KEEPING

Storing all the information I'd collected on the locations of gobbling birds, turkey sightings, roosts and turkey sign on paper topo maps used to be a rather formidable task. Eventually, I'd end up with a map covered with all sorts of markings, some obscuring others, the meaning of most long since forgotten. Thanks to modern technology, that job is now a whole lot easier.

Digital topo maps are now available on CD-rom programs like MapTech's Terrain Navigator. These programs allow you to store limitless information on turkey scouting in a well-organized format that is easily retrievable. You can place numbered symbols on the maps to indicate particular types of signs or occurrences. You can also store notes and reference them to the symbol and number.

All things considered, scouting is probably the most important aspect of successful turkey hunting. Again, the more time you spend scouting, the less you'll need to spend hunting. Even if spending time out of doors is more important than bagging a bird, scouting will give you another reason to do so. Now that you've located your bird, you're almost ready to go hunting. First, however, you need a little primer on turkey calling.

nine

CALLS & CALLING

nine

When I began turkey hunting, there wasn't nearly as much information available on how to do it, particularly in New England. And though I knew dozens of hunters, not a one had ever hunted turkeys. So, I had to learn on my own, with a little help on calling technique from a cassette by Ray Eye and Tom Stuckey, of H.S. Strut. Still, my best lesson in turkey calling came on the morning I killed my first gobbler.

It was during my third year of turkey hunting, and though I'd had a few close calls, I had yet to score. I vowed that if I didn't connect that spring, I would give the sport up altogether. I was already an obsessive deer and waterfowl hunter, and I felt I could do without one more compulsion. I guess I was meant to be a turkey hunter, because I got a little help from above that morning—directly above.

I'd scouted out a likely area one afternoon, and arrived just as light was breaking the next morning. I hadn't even reached my intended destination when I heard a distant gobble. My heart rate quickened. I took a bearing and raced off to cut the distance, stopping every hundred yards or so to relocate the gobbler. When I felt I'd gotten as close as I could, I began looking for a place to set up.

I found a big, comfortable-looking oak on the edge of a small cutover, nestled in against the trunk and began yelping on a diaphragm. I was already pumped up but I got really excited when the gobbler answered and started my way. Unfortunately, he hung up well out of sight. Still, things seemed to be going my way, and unbeknownst to me, something else was coming my way. Just then, a hen flew across the cut and landed in the tree directly over my head. I didn't realize it at the time, but in retrospect, she must have perceived me as a rival. Anyway, she soon began her own serenade. I imitated everything she did, and the more I called, the louder and more aggressively she called back.

The gobbler couldn't stand it. He broke the stalemate and started in. Not a moment too soon, the hen sailed off to parts unknown, leaving me the only hen calling in the woods. I continued to do exactly what the hen had just taught me, and before long I heard soft footfalls approaching on the dry leaves, followed by a deep, resonating "dooom" sound that I felt as much as heard. Instead of coming straight in, however, the gobbler circled to my left, and I had to wait until he was obscured behind a brush pile before I could quickly turn and reposition. When he stepped back into the open, I put a bead on my first gobbler and squeezed the trigger.

The basic premise of modern spring turkey hunting is to call a gobbler close enough to shoot. That sounds simple enough, but let me assure you it's not. In fact, it's complex enough that there have been dozens of books and videos, and thousands of magazine articles prepared on the subject. Part of the reason it's so complicated is that every encounter with a gobbler is unique. The same gobbler may react differently to different calls on different days, or even at different times on the same day. Still, knowing the generalities can get you started in the right direction. Proficient turkey calling first requires a basic understanding of the types of calling devices and the common vocalizations of turkeys. Let's begin with the latter.

CALLS

According to Lovett Williams, a renowned turkey biologist, the wild turkey's vocabulary consists of at least 30 distinct calls. Fortunately, you only need to know a half-dozen or so to hunt them effectively. The most common, most familiar to hunters, and most often imitated, is the "yelp," and there are several variations. The "plain yelp" is essentially a two-note *kee-yawk* sound. A typical rendition consists of repeating the two-note yelp five to seven times. If you can do this, you can kill a turkey, sometimes. While there is still some conjecture as to the exact meaning of this call, it seems to be a way for a hen to announce her presence and perhaps attract a mate. The "tree yelp" is a muted, one-note version, usually repeated only three or four times. This is a sound turkeys sometimes make while they're stirring on the roost, before flydown. The "assembly yelp" is just that, an assembly call, used by the hen to gather her brood flock, and is most often used in the fall. Finally, there is the "lost yelp." It is slightly louder and lower in pitch than the plain yelp, and may be repeated as many as 30 times. Turkeys are gregarious creatures, and while I wouldn't go so far as to say they get lonely, they may sound this call when looking for company.

The second basic, single-note call is the "cluck." It is a short, sharp note that sounds like its name. This call is often associated with contented feeding behavior, and may be a way for a flock of turkeys to keep track of one another in thick cover. Stringing together multiple, more excited clucks in rapid succession is called "cutting." This call may signal excitement or aggression. When suspicious, but not seriously alarmed, a turkey may utter a slightly louder, more rapid "pit-pit-pit." In effect, it's telling other nearby birds, "Something isn't quite right, so be on your toes." When a confirmed source of danger is identified, the turkey sounds an "alarm putt." This is a sharp, loud, one-note call, yet it has a ventriloqual quality, making it difficult to determine the direction of origin. To the turkey, it means danger. To the hunter, it means "game over."

The "cackle" is a combination of excited cutts and yelps, most often used as a turkey is flying down from the roost. It's almost as if the birds are announcing that they have "flown the coop," and are inviting others to join them. Or perhaps they're anxious about leaving the security of a comfortable pine, and need to release some of their anxiety as they do. Anyway, the cackle begins with several cutts as the bird flies down, then transitions into yelps when she hits the ground. On occasion, more often in the fall, turkeys may also cackle when flying up to roost in the evening.

The third basic vocalization is the "purr," which also sounds like its name. This also is a contented feeding call, and is considered by some as a spacing call—to keep other birds at a comfortable distance. It can be combined with a cluck, to produce the "cluck and purr." When used more aggressively, it becomes the "fighting purr" or "rattle." This is the sound made by fighting males. Like whitetail bucks, gobblers have a dominance hierarchy, and rivals often battle over breeding rights. When they do, this is the sound they make.

Another vocalization, used most often in the fall, is the "kee-kee." It consists of several short, high-pitched whistling notes, and is used by young birds that have not quite developed their voices. It's kind of like a teenager whose voice cracks as he goes through puberty. Poults may "kee-kee" any time, but become particularly vocal when separated from their flock. As the young birds become older and more vocally adept, they may break from the high-pitched kee-kees into yelps. This is called a "kee-kee-run."

A very different call is the "gobble." This is the mating call of the male turkey, which he uses to attract hens. In a typical mating scenario, the tom gobbles and struts to attract hens to him. The tom does most of his gobbling early in the morning, from the roost and shortly after flydown. However, toms may gobble any time of day, and will often gobble in response to a loud noise. I once heard a tom gobble at an overflying military helicopter. Once he started gobbling, it was easy to

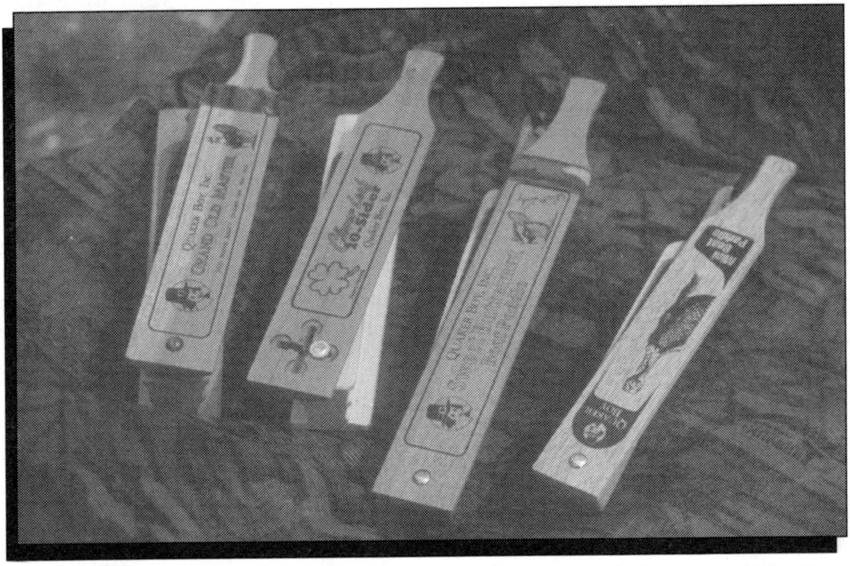

Box calls are relatively easy to use and loud, so their sound carries well. One drawback is that most require two hands to operate.

call him in. Unfortunately, it was 2:30 in the afternoon, and I had no permit. Still, it was good practice.

Another call, which I've already mentioned several times, is the spit-and-drum. This is a very soft, deep, bassy sound the gobbler makes while strutting. It is made by resonating air in his chest. This is a short-range sound, so if you hear it, you'd better be ready because the bird is close.

There is one more call you should at least be aware of. Though I've heard it numerous times in the field, I have never seen it referenced in any text. It is a very soft "pweet" that sounds like a drop of water falling into a puddle. I've most often heard it in association with contented feeding, or a lone hen just wandering about.

All of these calls can be imitated by one, or more, of the various types of calling devices that are available. The type of calling devices you can and should use to imitate the various turkey calls will depend on several things. Each has certain advantages and disadvantages. As with firearms, the key is to choose one that you can use most comfortably and effectively. Still, if you can master several, you'll have a distinct advantage.

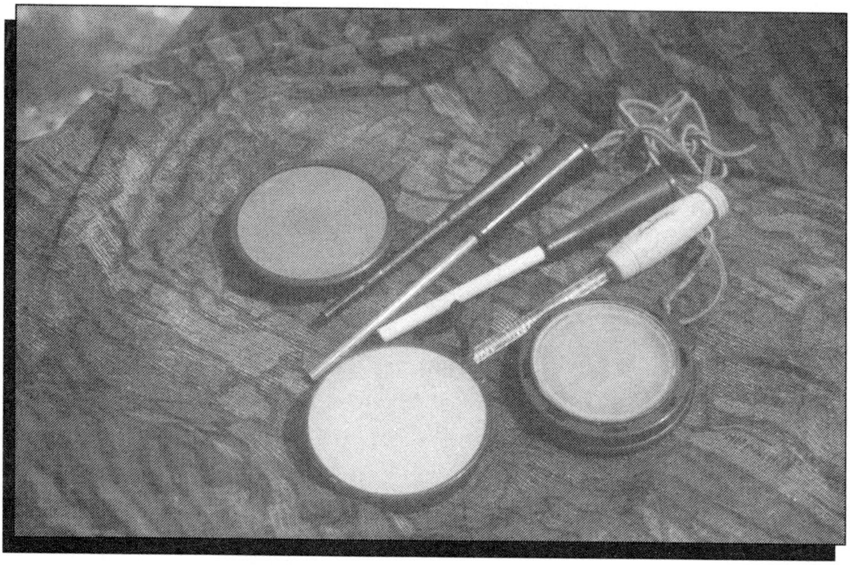

It's hard to beat the sweet sound of a good slate. With a little practice, slates are also easy to use, but like the box call, they require two hands.

CALLING DEVICES

Calling devices can be divided roughly into two groups: friction calls and mouth calls. Again, each has its pros and cons, depending on the situation and your own abilities

Friction Calls

Probably the oldest and most common type of friction call is the box call. The basic design consists of a wooden box, which forms a sound chamber, and a hinged paddle. You can make virtually all of the common turkey calls on the box. Yelps are made by drawing the paddle across the rail, or side of the box. Slow this motion down, and apply more pressure to get a purr. Cutts are made, either by striking the rail with the paddle, or holding the paddle on the rail with one thumb, and striking the paddle with your other hand.

The box call is loud, so the sound travels well. It's also easy to use. When calling loudly, you should be careful to grip the box and paddle lightly, with your fingertips. If you want to mute it—if you're working a close bird, for instance—do so by gripping the box firmly in your cupped hand. One of the biggest drawbacks of the box is that it requires two hands to operate. This ties up both your hands, and also requires movement. Turkeys have keen eyesight, and if you're hunting alone, you'll have to drop the call and pick up your gun long before you see the bird.

Another disadvantage is that wooden calls don't work when wet. Several solutions exist. Most manufacturers now make synthetic box calls that will work when wet. Lohman also makes a rosin solution that will waterproof any box call, and eliminate the need for chalking. I also know some hunters who keep their box calls in Ziploc bags, even when using them. Wooden box calls also require some maintenance; they must be chalked periodically to maintain proper friction between the paddle and box.

Another common friction call is the slate. This typically consists of a slate disc, mounted in a wooden bowl, or pot, though there are numerous variations in shapes and materials. Yelps and purrs are made by drawing a wooden peg across the surface. Drawing on the surface in a wide arc will create a yelp, while short, softer draws create purrs. You should grip the pot with your fingertips, using your cupped hand underneath as a sound chamber. Hold the peg, or striker, as you would a pencil, and draw it toward you. When making purrs and yelps, remember not to lift the striker off the slate; keep it in contact at all times. A cutt is made by picking or digging at the slate's surface with the striker.

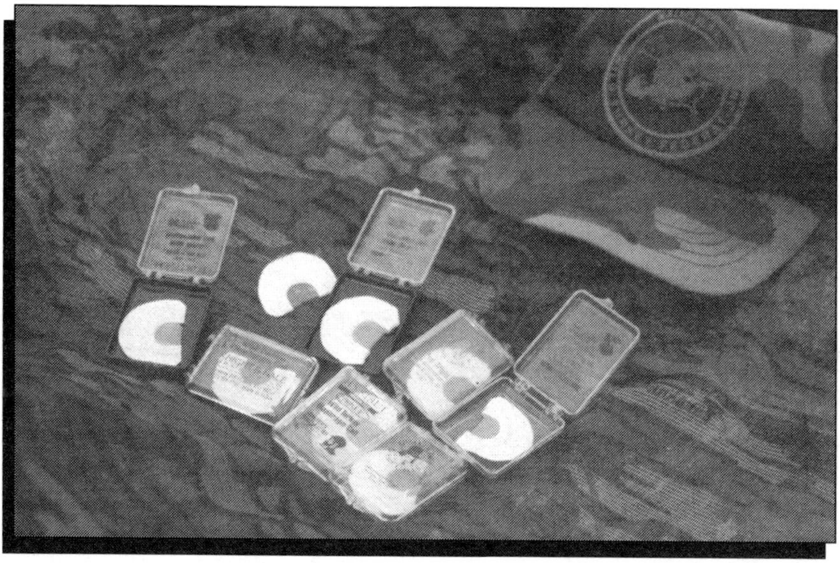

Diaphragm calls are the most difficult to master. However, they offer hands-free calling, and their versatility is limited only by your own calling skills.

Like the box, the slate requires two hands, and traditional slates also don't work when wet. However, many companies also make slates of various materials including plexi-glass, aluminum, copper and graphite; and strikers are made from a similar variety of materials. Some slates now come sectioned with two, three and even four different surfaces, and some strikers have interchangeable tips made of various materials. This gives you multiple options and allows you to change the tone or pitch, which can sometimes make a difference as to how a gobbler reacts to your calling.

Because slates work by friction, the surface must be maintained by sanding. If you think of your slate as a clock, sand from nine to three-o'clock, and call by drawing the striker across that grain, roughly from 12 to six o'clock. It's also important not to let your hands or fingers contact the slate's surface. Dirt and oils will reduce friction and deaden the sound. Both the box and slate are fairly easy to learn, and with a little practice, you'll be yelping, cutting and clucking like a real turkey.

Perhaps the best friction call for the beginner, and easiest to master is the push-pin, push-box or push-button call. It consists of a wooden box with a striker mounted inside. A wooden, spring-loaded dowel, with a small paddle attached, is then mounted through two holes in either end of the box. You can operate the call with one hand and sound is made by simply pushing the peg with one finger, which draws paddle across the striker. It is quieter than the box or slate, thus sound doesn't travel as far, but it only requires one hand, and very movement.

Like the box, it must be chalked, though some more recent versions come in a variety of synthetics that don't require chalking, and will work in the rain. One, Knight & Hale's Lonesome Hen, is also adjustable to

Using a gobble call while hunting is unsafe. However, it can sometimes make a good shock call for roosting birds in the evening.

make different tones. Some push-pins also come with clips or velcro straps that allow you to mount them directly on your gun barrel. By attaching a short length of string, one end to the peg and the other to your finger, you can work the call with one finger, while holding your gun up in the shooting position. Push-pin calls are great for purring, and several companies make dual, two-pin calls designed for imitating fighting purrs.

Mouth Calls

Mouth calls basically consist of tubes, wing bones and diaphragms. The latter is the most common type, but also the most difficult for many hunters to master. Some folks never can get the hang of it, but most can become proficient, with practice. While it is not as loud as a slate or box, it offers the distinct advantage of being hands-free.

The diaphragm consists of three parts: a metal, horseshoe-shaped frame, a similarly-shaped tape skirt and a latex reed. Press it against the roof of your mouth with your tongue, with the open end of the "U" facing forward. Sound is made by gradually easing the pressure on your tongue, while simultaneously blowing a burst of air across the reed. The first time you put a diaphragm in your mouth, it's gonna feel strange. And the first sound you make will probably be a lispy hiss. Don't despair; keep trying. When the reed begins to tickle the top of your tongue, you're making progress.

Next, try pressing the reed tighter with your tongue and blowing harder. Mouth the word "kee" as you do this. Eventually, you should get a high-pitched squeal. If it doesn't work right away, try this: Put the call in your mouth and whistle. Practice this until you become proficient. Next, as you begin your "kee," drop your jaw and tongue slightly, mouthing the word "yuk." As you speed up your "kee-yuk," it eventually becomes a yelp. You'll get a much more realistic sound if you can move your lower jaw as you do this.

A cluck is made with a soft burst of air across the reed, kind of just doing the "yuk" sound. Do this louder, and several times in repetition, and you're cutting. If it doesn't sound right at first, try rapidly mouthing "tut-tut-tut-tut." To kee-kee, push the reed tighter against your palate with your tongue and mouth the words "pee-pee-pee."

If you still can't master it, there's hope. Lohman makes a hand-held diaphragm called the pump-action yelper. It is a diaphragm mounted in a plastic tube. A piston-type bellows assembly provides the air. The down side is that it requires at least one hand to operate. They also make a smaller version that incorporates a diaphragm into a small tube that you simply blow into.

Diaphragms come in a variety of configurations, including single, double and triple reeds; stacked frames; and multiple reeds with a variety of cuts. Each will make a slightly different sound. A straight, single or double reed is probably a good choice for the beginner, as it provides a pure tone and is easier to use. As you become more proficient and experienced, you can try some of the other, multiple-reed calls to get a higher pitch or raspier sound.

With all of the above you can make the common calls: yelps, clucks, and purrs. If you just can't decide which call is best for you, bring one of each. This offers you greater flexibility under varying conditions, and more options for those fickle gobblers.

Two other types of mouth calls are the tube call and the wing-bone. With all of the other types of available calls, particularly some of the modern innovations, few hunters use these types anymore. Still, you might find them easier to use. With a little practice, both will render yelps and clucks. They require little maintenance, and only one hand to operate.

NON-TURKEY CALLS AND NON-CALL TURKEY SOUNDS

There are several other types of sounds you can use during the course of your hunt. One type is a "locator call." As previously mentioned, this is used to make a tom "shock gobble" and give away his location without focusing his attention toward you. Probably the most well-known is the barred owl call, most often used to locate a roosted tom the night before, or the morning of a hunt. To imitate it you give several successive hoots in a pneumonic cadence that goes: "Who cooks for you; who cooks for you all." If you can't do it with your voice, there are several commercial owl calls available. A coyote howl will sometimes serve the same purpose, and may even work better in heavily-hunted areas. After a while, turkeys become conditioned to owl calling and won't respond as readily. But if you hit 'em with the coyote howl, it may startle them because it's something they don't hear as often.

Later in the morning, if things are slow, you can also try to shock a bird using one of several sounds like a crow, peacock, coyote or pileated woodpecker. A standard "caw, caw" might shock a bird, but they hear crows all day. It's often more effective to sound like a very excited crow. You should also be on alert if you hear crows calling at something nearby. They will often swoop down and caw at turkeys.

If you, or a friend, are fortunate enough to bag a bird, cut off the outer part of the wing, with the primary feathers attached, dry it out and throw it in your vest. It can be used as a multipurpose turkey call. First, it can be used in conjunction with, or in place of, a fly-down cackle, to simulate one or more birds leaving the roost in the morning. Just slap it against a tree. An even more effective technique is using it to scratch in the leaves, simulating the sound of feeding turkeys. It adds more realism to your calling, and is sometimes more effective by itself, particularly on those wary old gobblers.

DIVERSITY

As mentioned in the previous chapter, it's always a good idea to carry multiple calls. If you only carry one box to save on weight and space, try to pick one with diverse features. Most boxes are designed so that striking each side renders a slightly different tone. You can also change the tone by adjusting the tension on the hinge screw, and Quaker Boy makes a box call with a slotted paddle that can be adjusted to five different positions, each rendering a different tone.

You can further increase your options by carrying several slates made of different materials, or split-face slates with two, three, even four different surfaces on a single call. You can also increase the diversity of an individual slate by carrying several strikers made of different materials, or one with interchangeable tips. Carrying a four-faced slate and a striker with three different tips gives you 12 different calls in one.

I also carry several different diaphragms that cover a range of tones, and because they take up so little space, I can carry more—typically four to six. Again, sometimes you have to find just the right tone or pitch to get a bird to gobble. Carrying several locator or shock calls also increases your calling options.

APPLICATION

Now that you are familiar with calls and calling devices, you need to know when and how to use them. A typical hunting scenario, if there is such a thing, might go something like this. You roost a bird the night before your hunt by going to a likely roost and owl hooting. The intent is to make a bird gobble, thus giving away his position. If he doesn't, you can always go back and try again just before dawn.

Assuming you've located a bird, sneak in as close as you can before dawn. Then set up and wait. You can give a few soft clucks, purrs or tree yelps, just to let him know you're there, but hold off on any real calling until he flies down, after daybreak. Turkeys seem to have better night vision than humans, and may fly down before full light. You don't want the bird to come in before you can see well enough to shoot, so hold off on your calling until it's light enough to clearly identify your target, and beyond. Begin your calling bout with a fly-down cackle, maybe accompanied with some wing flapping. Then start some yelping, or cutting.

What you should do next may depend on several things, but the most important is how the tom reacts to your calling. There are several different schools of thought on "taking a bird's temperature." I tend to be fairly aggressive, and if a bird gobbles every time I call, I call more. I'll get more assertive, with some aggressive cutting, and see how he reacts to that. If he gets lockjaw, I'll tone it down. Too much calling might intimidate a gobbler, particularly a subordinate tom or a jake, so it's probably better to err on the side of caution and be a little more conservative, until you gain more experience. I believe the key to aggressive calling is confidence.

Again, different hunters have different philosophies on how to handle a bird if he's coming to the call. If I have a bird really fired up, I like to keep him that way, so I pour it on. Others recommend you call just enough to keep his interest. You can switch to soft purrs as he gets closer, just to keep him on track, and remind him where you are. You can also do a little leaf rustling with your wing, to imitate feeding hens scratching in the leaves. More aggressive calling might bring him in faster, or it might not. Sometimes aggressive calling will cause a bird to hang up, and as my friend, George Mayfield says: "He may stand out there at 75 yards and gobble all day, but it ain't gonna do you no good."

Once the bird gets within about 50 yards, you should probably back off, or stop calling altogether, particularly if you have decoys out. If you're hunting in a field, you may even want to quit sooner. If you can see the bird at this point, and he's still coming, no more calling is necessary. If he seems to be veering off course, or stops to look around, you might want to reassure him with a few soft clucks or purrs. Again, I tend to be aggressive, and I've sometimes called birds until the moment I pulled the trigger. But that technique doesn't work for everyone, nor in every situation.

If a turkey "hangs up," or stops short of gun range and won't come any closer, it's decision time. This is one of the most frustrating aspects of turkey hunting, and where most hunts go awry. You can get more aggressive, hoping to budge him. Or, you can stop calling, hoping to pique his curiosity. Sometimes you just gotta roll the dice and see what comes up.

It is said that succes occurs when opportunity meets preparation. After two frustrating days of hunting, I was doing a little mid-morning scouting when I spotted this New Hampshire tom. I was prepared.

Failure to draw a permit in Maine's lottery forced me to become a registered Maine guide, just so I could be in the woods every spring. My first client, Bill Bayreuther, took his first turkey 15 minutes into the 1997 Spring Season.

You can apply the techniques you learn hunting New England turkeys just about anywhere, and vice versa. George Mayfield flew up from Alabama to join me on a Green Mountain gobbler hunt, and was not dissapointed.

Sometimes you get lucky. My first spring gobbler with a bow was a real limb-hanger, and turned out to be the Massachusetts state archery record.

Mark Luthman and I learned how to hunt turkeys together. Despite his occasional unorthodox methods, he has become an accomplished turkey hunter.

After several frustrating years of failing to draw a permit in Maine, Jim Eshelman's name finally came up and he tagged out on opening day.

Spring comes early for New England's turkeys and the mating season often begins while there's still snow on the ground.

The mating display of the wild turkey is a magnificent promenade. He begins by puffing up his body feathers. He simultaneously lifts his tail and spreads the feathers to form a full fan, while lowering his wings so the outer primaries drag on the ground.

Perhaps one of the best things about turkey hunting is being able to share the experience with friends. Todd Kalter helped me call in my first Green Mountain gobbler.

Thanks to the efforts of state biologists, dedicated volunteers and support from the National Wild Turkey Federation, we now have vigorous turkey populations throughout New England.

Keen-eyed and wary, the wild turkey presents a daunting challenge to the hunter, and any bird, regardless of weight or beard length, is a trophy.

Military surlpus woodland camo was still the most popular camo pattern when took my first Maine turkey.

Either way, sit tight, especially if he stops gobbling. A tom will often stop gobbling, go into strut, and close the last 50 to 70 yards silently. If you can see the bird, that will help you plan a response. If not, freeze! Hold perfectly still and listen for approaching footsteps, or the spit-and-drum of a strutting tom. Minutes will seem like hours, but the minute you stand up to see where that bird went, you'll hear his alarm putt, and see a flash of disappearing feathers.

This is when patience becomes the turkey hunter's greatest asset. If a bird goes silent, a good rule of thumb is: If you're not sure you've waited long enough, you haven't. If you think you have, wait at least another 20 to 30 minutes. If you're sure you've waited long enough, sit tight for another ten to 15 minutes. It's better to let the bird lose interest and walk away than to risk spooking him. You can always come back later and try again if you haven't scared him off.

This is also when having multiple calls can be helpful. A higher pitch might bring in a two-year-old, but an old limb-hanger may hold out for the mature voice of a raspy old hen. A tom that already has hens may not come to your call, but if you can irritate the dominant hen enough by imitating her exactly in tone and cadence, she might come, and bring her boyfriend with her.

Competition sometimes works better than seduction, and when a henned-up tom won't respond to your sweet, seductive hen calls, you can use a low-pitched raspy call to make jake yelps. A higher-pitched call that allows you to break into kee-kee runs may work better on jakes, who are timid from being run off by more dominant birds, and are merely seeking companionship.

Incidentally, you should never be ashamed of shooting a jake. They'll sometimes gobble and strut just like a tom, and some of my most exciting hunts ended with me pulling the trigger on a precocious short-beard. Taking jakes is also biologically sound. They have no real role in the breeding ritual, and there is usually a surplus of them in any given spring. They also taste just as good as a tom.

FIGHTING PURRS

Another tactic that works, on occasion, is the fighting purr or rattle. Like rattling for deer, this simulates the sound of rival males sparring for dominance. It consists of loud, aggressive purrs, often accompanied with clucks and wing-slapping. It should be considered a last-ditch effort, as you're just as likely to scare birds as call them in. Still, when the turkey's mood is right, it works.

I once got spotted by a jake as I was walking through some open hardwoods. Fortunately, he wasn't sure what I was. He froze, and so did I. Ever so slowly, I eased into a sitting, shooting position, and began calling. I got no reaction so I got more aggressive—still no reaction. So, I figured, what the heck. I snuck out my fighting purrs and worked them for all they were worth. The jake's head turned red, white and blue, and he marched down the hill toward me. Unfortunately, at the last second he veered behind a fallen tree, and I never got a shot.

CALLING BLIND

Turkey calling techniques have evolved tremendously over the last several decades. If you doubt that, ask someone who's been turkey hunting for more than 20 years what the recommended technique was when they started hunting. More than likely they'll say something to the effect of: "Yelp three times on a box call; then sit and wait a half an hour."

Nobody really knows why, but there are some days when the birds just won't gobble, and you'd swear there isn't a turkey within ten miles. When that happens, it may be a good time to go back to old ways: pick a likely spot, make yourself comfortable and just yelp on a box call every 15 or 20 minutes.

Where you call is much more important than how you call, and your effectiveness will relate to how much scouting you've done. We'll discuss more about where to set up in the next chapter. The best caller in the world may not be able to lure in a bird if he's calling from the wrong location. Contrarily, if you're in an area birds use on a regular basis, you could almost go without calling. Again, with silent birds, as with hung-up birds, it can be extremely advantageous to carry and use several different types of calls. Experiment until you find something that gets a gobble.

TROLLING

Another modified version of calling blind is sometimes referred to as "trolling." Essentially, you're blind calling on the move, trying to elicit a shock gobble. As you travel along, stop every 100 to 200 yards, and call. Some hunters prefer to use a non-turkey call for this technique. Owls calls work best during twilight hours. Later in the morning, you should switch to another type, like a crow or woodpecker call. Carrying both is better because, like the tom that will gobble at one slate and not another, some birds will react to one type of shocker but not another. The advantage of using shock calls is that you can get a bird to gobble without attracting his attention to you. This allows you to move closer, or move to a better set-up position before you begin calling the bird in. Otherwise, he may come to the call too fast and catch you out of position—I speak from experience.

When using this technique, extreme caution is advised. Move along slowly and quietly, looking and listening all the time, much as you would if you were still-hunting for deer. There may be other hunters in the woods nearby. You don't want to interfere if they're working a bird, and you don't want them mistaking you as game. Also, you may be able to catch sight or sound of turkeys quietly feeding along before they spy you. Stop frequently and listen for the sounds of feeding birds or a distant gobble.

USE, TUNING & CARE OF CALLS

Most, if not all, turkey calls are made so they're ready to work out of the box. However, some may need a little tweaking, particularly after the break-in period. And with others, you can enhance their effectiveness with a little fine-tuning. In time, most will need a little maintenance, and the more attention you devote to them, the longer they'll last.

Mouth diaphragm calls are designed to fit the "average" person's mouth. However, everyone's mouth is different in shape and size. If you have trouble fitting the call in your mouth, you may need to trim the skirt with a pair of scissors. Trim a little bit at a time until it fits tightly without letting any air pass. You can also bend the frame slightly to better fit the roof of your mouth. Bending the frame will also change the call's pitch.

When you're finished with your mouth calls for the season, store them in a cool, moist location, like your refrigerator, to prolong between-season life. You can also peg the reeds by placing toothpicks between individual reeds. Before using them in subsequent seasons, rinse them in a solution of mouthwash and water to kill any leftover bacteria. Before I learned this trick, I used to come down with a nasty sinus infection every year around the beginning of turkey season. You may also want to do this periodically, throughout the season.

Friction calls often require repeated maintenance throughout the season. Make sure you keep the underside of your box call lid well-chalked with greaseless chalk. This is a very important point. Some chalks, like blackboard chalk, contain grease that will clog the pores in the wood grain. You should also carry a small strip of sandpaper or emery cloth and a patch of Scotchbrite to keep your slates and strikers roughened up. In both cases, never touch the friction surface of your calls with bare hands as you could transfer grease and oils, reducing friction and sound.

If your box call starts sounding flat, even after chalking, it may need a little reconditioning. Sand the paddle very lightly with a fine (100-grit) sandpaper to open up the grain of the wood. Then chalk it and see how it sounds. You can also tune your box by turning the hinge screw in or out. Do this in small increments until you find the best sound.

Rather than tuning slate calls, you can find various locations on the call that render different tones. For example, the edges produce a higher pitch than the middle of the call. Unlike synthetic slates, true slates are not completely flat, and various locations on the slate's surface will render slightly different tones. Every true slate has a "sweet spot" that renders the best tone. Once you find it, notch the rim of your call so you can position it in your hand to find the sweet spot by feel.

Now you know everything you need to know about turkey hunting, right? Not really, but most of the rest can only come with experience. Still, you have enough knowledge to go afield with confidence, and that is the second most important characteristic of a turkey hunter. Let's go hunting.

ten

THE SETUP

ten

It had been an especially busy morning, and I had already worked three different birds by 7:30, but had nothing to show for it. As I climbed a small ridge I heard a distant gobble, just about at the limit of my hearing. The bird had to be close to a quarter-mile away, and I knew he might quit gobbling at any moment, but there was nothing going on nearby. So I headed off in his direction.

To get to the bird I had to traverse several finger ridges, and it took me a while to cover the distance. Every time I went down between ridges, I'd lose track of the bird, and had to stop frequently to relocate his gobble. To add to my troubles, I had to circumnavigate a beaver pond, which slowed me down even more. When I finally topped the last ridge, I was relieved to hear not one, but two gobblers.

Between us lay a big hardwood swamp. Ordinarily I would have gone around it. But it was getting late in the morning, and I was worried the gobbling would cease; so I headed straight across the swamp. I knew there was an open field on the far side, and my plan was to sneak up to the field edge and try to call the birds over.

My hastily-prepared plan began to unravel when, halfway across the swamp, I suddenly noticed the two toms strutting in the field at a distance of about 200 yards. Luckily, they hadn't seen me yet, but between us there wasn't enough cover to allow me to sneak any closer. To make matters worse, they were on the far side of a barbed wire fence, uphill from me, and I was standing ankle deep in swamp water. I was experienced enough to know that you can't call a turkey through a fence, downhill or across water, let alone all three. But I was also green enough to try anyway; I really had no choice.

I crawled up into the roots of a wind-thrown swamp maple, propped my gun up on my knee and began yelping as loudly as I could on a diaphragm. If I hadn't seen it with my own eyes I would never have believed what happened next. The nearest bird quit gobbling, folded up his fan and started downhill. He squeezed under the barbed wire, then proceeded on a circuitous route around the puddles of ankle deep water, but still generally in my direction. I wish I could say I tumbled him neatly, but my first shot went a little high and it took a follow up to do him in.

Try to set up with your back against a tree at least as wide as your shoulders. This provides better concealment, helps to break up your outline and will protect your back in the event you or your decoys are mistaken for game.

THE BASICS

That's probably about as poor an example of how to set up on a bird as I can imagine. But it shows how much you can get away with, on rare occasions. If you're willing to entrust your turkey hunting success to the vagaries of fate, you can skip this chapter. If, on the other hand, you want to hedge your bets, you might want to read on. There's a lot you can do in terms of where, when and how you set up that can significantly increase your chances of success.

Let's begin with some basic guidelines. Notice I didn't use the term "rules." That's because for every rule there is an exception, and turkeys don't read the rules anyway. Still, they follow some general patterns.

Deciding how much cover to leave in front of yourself is a trade-off. Too much cover could interfere with your shot. Not enough and you're liable to get busted by a sharp-eyed bird. With good camouflage and patience you won't need as much.

When moving in on a roosted bird, get as close as you can. How close is that? My father had a saying about tightening nuts and bolts: "Tight is tight; too tight is broken." The same adage works for turkeys, too. Until you've busted a few birds out of the roost, you really won't know how close you can get. Still, if you stay on the conservative side, 100 yards is a good general rule-of-thumb. Of course, that can vary with habitat. A hundred yards may be way too tight in early spring hardwoods; or, you may be able to get even closer if the leaves are quiet and the underbrush dense.

Turkeys are easier to call uphill. I don't know why, but it seems to be true. In hilly terrain, if at all possible, try to set up above, or at least at the same level as the gobbler. They will sometimes come downhill to a call, but your odds of calling a bird uphill are much greater.

Set up with your back against a tree at least as wide as your shoulders. There are two reasons for this. One, it provides better concealment from birds approaching either from the front or the rear. Two, it will protect your back in the event you or your decoys are mistaken for game. Also, try to set up with the sun at your back. It will put any bird approaching from the front at a disadvantage.

How much cover you leave or place directly in front of you is a matter of personal preference. If you're the fidgety type, probably the more the better. This will allow you some freedom to move, but not much. However, that same cover may also get in the way when it's time to shoot, obscuring your vision or preventing a shot. I prefer to have little or no cover in front of me so I have a clear, open shot when the time comes. My gun is usually up on my knee and pointed toward the bird long before I'm ready to shoot.

This brings up another point. You don't want to be directly facing an approaching gobbler. If you're right handed, sit with your left shoulder toward the bird. This will give you more room to maneuver your gun if the bird moves to your right. Do the opposite if you're left-handed.

It's also helpful if you can pick a location with at least 20 or 30 yards of good, open visibility in front of you. You must be able to clearly identify your target, and you don't want anything that will interfere with your shot pattern. A gobbler may also be reluctant to enter thick brush, so give him a clear path to you.

IN THE FIELD

I've heard many a veteran hunter say that field birds are harder to kill. I don't know why, because over the years I've killed the majority of my birds in fields. Of course, I've sometimes had to resort to some rather unorthodox methods to do so. Hunting fields has its advantages and disadvantages, but knowing them can help you decide where, when and how to set up.

Decoys can be particularly important when hunting field birds, as it give them something to associate with the sound of your calling. How you position them can also be important.

First and foremost, you should be where the birds want to go. You may be able to pull birds to any point along a field edge, but if you position yourself where they normally travel, that will be a lot easier to do. This is another area where scouting is especially important. If you have the opportunity, watch the field you intend to hunt and make notes on where the birds travel. Then you'll know where to set up.

DECOYS

One of the major disadvantages of hunting field birds is that because they're in the open, they can see a long way. They can hear your calls, but if they don't see the source, they're often hesitant to come. That's why decoys are so important. Due to the long distance visibility, they can give you an edge. If I know I'll be hunting fields, I always bring decoys, and I've developed some innovative deployment tactics.

The position, pose and sex of your decoys are all important. A typical decoy flock, at least the way they're sold, consists of three: one jake and two hens. When using this trio, I always try to place the jake closest to me, well-within gun range, and put the hens another ten yards or so farther out. My experience has been that the tom will almost always approach the jake decoy first, trying to separate him from the hens.

Seeing a potential rival with hens appeals to the jealous nature of a tom. But seeing a jake or another tom breeding a hen absolutely drives him wild. Several decoy manufacturers now make decoys that can be positioned in the breeding posture, with the jake on top of the hen. If you don't own them, you can position your own decoys in the same way. A hen squats to be bred so stake a hen decoy at ground level. Then stake a jake on top, and slightly to the rear. You'll be amazed how effective this posture can be. Sometimes, even a single hen placed in the breeding position will work better than an upright hen.

Another thing I try to do is face my decoys in the direction I want an approaching tom to travel. Consider this: You see someone you want to talk to, and they're standing on the other side of a large room. If he's facing you, you may try to catch his attention, and wait for him to come to you. If you see he's headed the other way though, you're more likely to cross the room to get to him before he leaves. While I don't believe turkeys go through the same reasoning process, I do believe they react similarly, based on which way the decoys are facing.

You should also consider the turkey's direction of approach. Most hunters place their decoys directly in front of them. However, if the tom approaches straight on, he'll be looking directly at the decoys and you. Even if you don't move, he may notice something out of place. You're better off placing the decoys slightly off to one side, to your left if you're right-handed and to your right if left-handed. If you think the turkey will approach from one side or the other, place your decoys on the far side, leading him past and in front of you.

As previously mentioned, where you set up can be critical, and the key to hunting field birds is visibility. Whenever possible, try to set up on a high spot, so your decoys can be seen from any direction, and from a long way off.

Another good setup position is at the point, where a finger of woods juts into a field. With a flat woodline at your back, you have 180 degrees of visibility. Set up on a point, and you and your decoys will have greater visibility.

FLOCK 'EM

There are two types of field birds that present a particularly daunting challenge. One is a henned-up gobbler—a tom with a harem of hens. He already has what he wants, and even the best caller in the world isn't likely to pull him into a setup of two or three decoys. However, turkeys are gregarious by nature, and if you can pull in the hens, the gobblers will follow. Sometimes a larger flock of decoys—six or seven—provides enough incentive to pull the birds over.

The other almost impossible to kill turkey is the one that won't come near the edge. Nature has selected for this behavior because its easy for turkeys to see any approaching danger. Some birds, particularly in heavily hunted areas, will fly from the roost and glide into the middle of a big field. Or, they'll approach the field cautiously. Then, once they're in the open, they head for the middle, where they may spend hours strutting around. If and when they do exit, it will almost never be in the same location.

Such predisposed birds can be tough, but even they are not un-killable. If there is any cover or structure at all out in the field, use it as a blind. You can use something as simple as a piece of farm equipment, hay bales or a small patch of brush. If the grass is long enough, you could even try a layout blind. The possibilities are limited only by your own imagination.

IN THE WOODS

Setting up on birds in the woods is often much easier. In addition to setting up above a bird and with an opening in front of you, there are other ways to improve your set up in the woods. For example, if you're in hilly terrain, try to set up on a bench. Then, set your decoys so any bird approaching from downhill will not be able to see them until he is within range, or close to it. Woods roads also make for good set up locations. They offer you and the turkeys better visibility, and turkeys tend to travel them. Loggers will often seed these roads to prevent erosion, unwittingly creating food plots and strut zones.

Being familiar with the terrain in the area you hunt is also important. If at all possible, try to avoid setting up with any obstacles like fences, streams or wetlands between you and the bird. They may cross them, but it is less likely. You may even be able to use these obstacles to steer a bird toward you.

Every turkey is unique and every encounter is different. Still, if you know the basics you can adapt them to most any situation. Better insight into where to set up will come with experience.

eleven

ADVANCED TACTICS

eleven

Strong wind and heavy rain had prevented me from roosting a bird the night before Opening Day. Nonetheless, I had seen some birds that afternoon in an area I was very familiar with, so I figured they wouldn't be far off come daybreak. My plan was to arrive just before gobbling time, wait for the birds to announce their location, then move in and set up.

It was cool and drizzling, so the birds were a little late in sounding off, giving me plenty of time to slip in close to where I suspected they'd roosted. My hunch paid off when two gobblers chimed from the treetops several hundred yards away. I eased in a tad closer, sat down and began my calling bout. The two toms answered my calls obligingly, but remained up in the trees for some time. Still, things seemed to be going according to plan, until birds began pitching out of the trees. The toms weren't alone, and the instant her feet touched the soggy earth, a raspy old hen began yelping aggressively at them. I called back, but that only aggravated her. She wasn't about to share, and hastily led the gobblers in the opposite direction.

The toms were obviously henned-up, so I made the difficult decision to leave them and come back later. After a couple hours of trolling around the silent woods, I eventually made it back to the roost area and, just as I'd suspected, the toms had also returned. The game was back on.

One tom gobbled back at my calls, and moved a bit closer, eventually hanging up out beyond a hundred yards. Leaving the birds and then coming back had worked, to a point. Now it was time to try another stubborn gobbler trick.

I did a long bout of aggressive yelping and cutting that really fired that gobbler up. Then I shut up. For ten agonizingly long minutes I sat silently, scanning the woods for any sight of the gobbler, but he too had

Taking this gobbler concluded one of my most memorable hunts. It took the better part of a morning and several specialized tactics to finally lure him into gun range.

gone silent. When I finally broke the silent stand-off, the bird gobbled back immediately, this time from much closer. But he hung up again, just on the other side of a thick grove of hemlocks.

He was in a strut zone, a place where he'd strut and gobble, trying to attract a female to his position. By listening for his gobbles, I could track his progress as he repeatedly moved to within about 100 yards, then paced back to 150 or so. The next time the bird hit the far point, I made my final move, creeping another 30 yards closer. When the tom gobbled again from 70 yards away, I yelped back. Closing that last critical distance did the trick. The tom broke out of his strut zone and sauntered in. As soon as he cleared the hemlocks he was in range, and shortly afterward, was in my vest.

That bird provided one of my most exciting and challenging hunts. We did battle for the better part of that morning, and it took the combination of three specialized tactics to eventually bring him to the gun. Had I encountered that situation a few years earlier, I likely would have either given up or blown it, because I lacked the experience and knowledge of how to deal with tough toms.

Aggressive calling does sometimes work, but you've got to be able to read a bird, listen to how he reacts to your calling and adjust accordingly.

If you could choreograph the perfect hunt, it would probably go something like this. You roost a bird the night before your hunt. The next morning, you slip in under cover of darkness and set up close to the roost. Just as the light breaks the treetops, the tom begins gobbling and you begin yelping. He answers to your every call, flies down, struts into your decoys, and "boom!" The hunt is over.

That does happen, but not very often. More often than not, something goes awry with our best laid plans. That's when we need to fall back on our arsenal of advanced tactics (ad-lib). Knowing how to make the various turkey vocalizations is certainly an asset, but to be more successful in difficult situations, we have to know when, where and how to apply those calls as well. We also need to know when not to call at all, when to move and when to sit tight, and the more tricks we know, the better are our odds for success. What follows are some of the advanced tactics I've learned from my own experiences, as well as those of some of turkey hunting's upper classmen.

PASSIVE-AGGRESSIVE CALLING

To call or not to call, that is the question. In my turkey calling seminars, I tell students that the biggest mistake novice turkey hunters make is calling too much; the second biggest mistake is not calling enough. Success comes with just the right amount. But how do we know what that is? When I started hunting, I was always reluctant to call too much, mostly because I lacked confidence. I've since learned that aggressive calling can often turn the tables on a reluctant gobbler. However, too much calling might just as easily spook him. Several factors can help solve the passive-aggressive calling riddle.

A good rule of thumb is: Let the gobbler be your guide. Take his temperature. How he reacts to your calling will reveal a lot about how much you should call. My advice is: If he responds every time you call, hammer him with more calling. If he double and triple gobbles and cuts you off, cut him off. Fire him up. If, on the other hand, he shuts up or shies away, ease up and be patient.

One of the most aggressive callers I've ever hunted with is Brad Harris. Brad is Vice President of public relations for Outland Sports. He's also an accomplished contest caller and experienced turkey hunter. While hunting with Brad one morning in Kansas, I watched him meticulously work three reluctant toms. They'd gobble when he called, but they just wouldn't budge. Brad unloaded his arsenal on them, switching between slates, box calls and diaphragms, calling nearly non-stop. It took over an hour, but he eventually pulled them in to my gun. I learned a valuable lesson that day about aggressive calling.

I learned a bit about passive calling from another friend, George Mayfield, owner of The Roost in Alabama. George has been hunting gobblers since he was knee-high to a grasshopper, and now guides in Alabama, Mississippi and Missouri, and frequently judges several national calling competitions.

I invited him up one spring to hunt Green Mountain gobblers with me in Vermont. Being the local "expert," I felt pressured to produce, but after three hard days of hunting, he'd put me to shame. We'd both worked birds every day but he had two and I had none. I finally swallowed my pride and asked how he did it. These birds are still "henned-up," he said. "You can't call too aggressively. I call just enough to keep track of where they are, then I move around to get in front of them."

A tom with hens can be extremely difficult to call in. However, if you switch your attention to the hen, and call her in, the tom will follow.

HENNED-UP BIRDS

One of the biggest obstacles most turkey hunters will face is dealing with henned-up birds, toms who have already gathered their harem, and are in no hurry to leave them for the proverbial "bird in the bush." Timing your hunt is one way to avoid this obstacle. Most seasons are set to begin after the majority of hens have been bred, and the later the season gets, the fewer hens are around to interfere. However, a cold spring can delay mating, leaving surplus hens around late into the season. Furthermore, we don't all have the luxury of being able to hunt when we want. Also, as you get later into the season, there are fewer toms around, too, and remaining birds may become call-shy from prolonged hunting pressure.

So how to you overcome a henned-up tom? One way is to try to avoid dominant birds and switch your attention to satellite toms. During the breeding season, turkeys are a lot like elk. One dominant tom does most of the breeding, while potential rivals constantly tag along, hoping to get a little side action. These satellite toms are often easier to call, but may require a little finesse. Rather than aggressive calling, try calling softly, maybe with a few light clucks and purrs.

Think of yourself as a young hen who wants to join the flock, but is timid.

If that doesn't work, you could switch to jake calling. Jakes are the spike bucks of the turkey world. They're like teenage boys; they have all the right equipment, but they don't quite know how to use it. They also know they're at the bottom of the pecking order. A jake's yelp is like a hen's, but louder, coarser and somewhat deeper in tone. These younger birds, though excited, are still aware of their social position. When yelping, they may often break into kee-kees. Like a herd bull chasing off satellites, a tom may come charging in if he hears a subordinate calling *his* hens. Incidentally, this call, like the fighting purr, is also murder on younger toms and jakes.

FIGHTING PURRS

Fighting purrs can be a very effective calling technique when used under the right circumstances. The theory is the same as rattling bucks: By imitating the sound of dominant rivals, you'll attract other males. Jimmy Gaccione, who is a good friend and a pro-staffer for Outland Sports, related an excellent example.

He was guiding a group of writers one spring in an area where the birds had been hunted hard, and just weren't cooperating. He and his hunter, an anonymous editor, settled in to an area where the turkeys had been particularly uncooperative. He decided to forgo the usual yelping, and went straight to fighting purrs—purring, clucking and slapping his false turkey wing with all the might he could muster. When he was done, the editor looked at him incredulously. "Now everyone knows we're here," was all Jim said. Within minutes, a silent tom entered the field and started their way. Jimmy had all he could do to contain the astonished editor until the bird was within range.

HEN CALLING

Another way to overcome a henned-up tom is by targeting not the boss tom, but the boss hen. Hens also have a pecking order, and if you can fire up the dominant hen, she might come your way. She will likely be the most vocal bird in a flock. Imitate her tone, cadence and volume as much as you can, and remember my advice for aggressively calling a tom. If she cuts you off, it's working. Pour it on. Keep calling, and soon she'll start heading your way to see who's trying to upstage her. Along with her will come the rest of the flock, including the tom. And satellite males may just be the first ones to arrive.

Of course, there's always the risk that she'll do just like the hen in the opening passage to this chapter, and lead the gobbler straight away. If that happens, you have two options. One is to do what I did—back off and try again later. The other is to try and circle around, ahead of the flock, and intercept them. You still probably won't be able to call them in, and will have to rely on pre-hunt scouting to speculate at where they're headed.

PLANT A SEED

We'd all like to kill our birds just after they've left the roost. But again, it seldom works out that way. More often, the bird bails out and hangs up, or heads off for parts unknown. You can overcome the latter scenario in a couple of ways. One is to devote the time needed to pattern a particular bird. However, not many hunters have the time, or motivation to dedicate several days to such a task. Furthermore, interference from another hunter could easily upset your gobbler's routine, assuming he has one.

I learned another trick from Vermonter Mark Scott. Mark works for the Fish & Wildlife Department, and is a veteran turkey hunter. His technique depends on first locating a roosted gobbler in the evening. Then, he slips in to where he plans to set up the next morning. With a turkey wing, a hat or a piece of canvas, he simulates the sound of a hen flying to roost, while also doing a fly-up cackle. Finally, he gives a few soft tree calls. Turkeys have small brains, but they seem to have excellent memories. That tom will remember where he heard that hen fly to roost. The next morning, he'll be off the roost and on his way to you at first light. And you'll be waiting for him.

TAG TEAM

If you hunt with a partner, you're at a decided advantage, particularly if you're dealing with a hung-up bird. One technique that sometimes works is to have the caller back off a ways, leaving the silent shooter between him and the bird. The theory is that the tom senses the hen has lost interest and moved on. Both are playing "hard-to-get." The tom still won't come all the way to the caller, but he may close the distance enough to get within range of the shooter.

PATIENCE-PLUS

The basic premise of spring turkey hunting is to find a gobbling tom and call him in. This, of course, requires a cooperative subject. No one really knows why, but there are some days when the woods are dead quiet; the turkeys just won't gobble. You can try to raise a shock gobble. But that often ends with frustration, and tired feet. An alternate tactic is to pick a spot, plant yourself and just keep calling. If you've done your scouting well, sooner or later a tom will come within hearing, and your calling might just be enough to lure him in. There are no hard and fast rules, but a two or three-minute calling bout every 15 minutes or so is adequate. In between bouts, be still and quiet, and listen for footfalls on the leaves. On those quiet days, a tom is very likely to come in silently. A good many novices have killed respectable birds this way, and I know a few savvy veterans who regularly use this very effective technique.

SHUT UP

Sometimes the best calling is no calling at all. While some of my colleagues would disagree, I believe that birds become call-shy in heavily hunted areas. On several occasions, while hunting the second or third week of the season, I've had vocal birds shut up and disappear at the first sound of a turkey call. I was guiding a hunter on one such occasion, and we'd worked birds for two days with similar results. No matter where we set up, as soon as they heard my calls, they went mum, and away from me. On day three we devised a simple plan: I agreed not to call.

We sneaked in before daylight, as close to the roost as we could get, set out our decoys and waited. When the chorus of tree-top gobbles began, it took all the self control I could muster not to call back. Soon we heard the flapping of wings against tree branches, followed by soft footsteps. Within minutes, the birds were in the decoys, and my hunter filled his tag.

NON-VOCAL & NON-TURKEY CALLING

In addition to yelps, clucks and purrs, turkeys make a variety of other sounds the hunter can put to good use. For instance, by imitating the sound of wings flapping at fly-down time you're telling a tom the hens have flown down and they're waiting for him. This can be done with a wing, a hat, or one of several commercially available wing simulators. You can also use your wing to scratch gently in the leaves, simulating the sound of feeding hens. This tactic is sometimes deadly on hung-up toms.

If the woods are silent and you decide to go the trolling route, you're better off trying to locate a bird using something other than a turkey call. You don't want to give away your position until you're ready to set up and begin calling. You're trying to elicit a shock gobble, startling the bird into gobbling. Under the right conditions, most any loud noise will work. The more popular ones include crow, woodpecker and coyote calls. When using a crow call, don't sound like just any crow; that's a common sound. Try to sound like a crow caught in the talons of a great-horned owl. As discussed earlier, I prefer a woodpecker call because fewer hunters use it, and it is more of a shock. Coyote calls seem to work better around twilight, as this is when most coyotes howl. However, they and owl calls will sometimes work throughout the day.

CONCLUSION

These are but a few of the more advanced tactics you can use on troublesome toms. You'll no doubt learn more of your own as you become more experienced. Sometimes they won't work. Other times, however, one or more may be the only thing that will bring in a reluctant gobbler. As you become more experienced, you'll learn which ones to apply under various circumstances. That knowledge won't come without a good bit of trial and error though, so don't be afraid to push the envelope and try new techniques when your hunt doesn't go according to plan. You'll blow a few opportunities in the process, but ultimately you'll be a better turkey hunter for it. Many of the hunts from which I learned the most ended without killing a bird.

twelve

BOWHUNTING

twelve

Despite my 3-D leafy camo suit, I felt naked as a newborn. When the big gobbler topped the rise in the long field, he was 70 yards away. I'd mis-calculated his direction of approach, and now there was nothing between us but air. Bow resting on my boot, I squinted my eyes and peered through quivered arrows as I watched his slow progress toward me. Though the gobbler looked at me suspiciously several times, he continued closing the distance, alternately fanning his broad tail, gobbling, and picking at a stray insect as he approached the single hen decoy.

At 25 yards, he stretched out his neck and let out a tremendous gobble that nearly bowled me over. My arms and legs trembled uncontrollably from fatigue and excitement, and I feared he'd detect me at any moment. As a last resort, I had to close my eyes to settle myself. Fortunately, when I opened them, he was finally moving to my left. A few more steps and I would be concealed behind the bole of a big oak. As soon as I was, I drew back on my bowstring, still kneeling. I checked my anchor point and sight, then ever so slowly, eased out from behind the tree at full draw. There he was, standing broadside, and in full strut. I quickly settled the pin on his wing butt and took a deep breath.

I don't remember releasing, but the next sound I heard was a loud *thwack* as my arrow struck the bird dead-center. He cartwheeled, then tore off, the arrow still protruding from his side. Thirty yards away I found my prize, an old limbhanger that sported a 10 1/2-inch beard and 1 1/4-inch spurs—a magnificent specimen by any standards, but especially rewarding for a bowhunter.

Trying to take an old gobbler with a gun is tough enough, but doing it with a bow might seem downright impossible. First, we must go against a tom's very nature by luring him to us. Next, we have to draw on a bird who's keen eyesight is unmatched among game animals.

Then, we fire a projectile that travels slower than the bird's reflexes can react to the twang of a bowstring. It is a daunting challenge at best. Still, the tools and techniques for hunting with bow and gun are not significantly different. Those who have already hunted turkeys with a gun, or deer with a bow, need only to modify what they've learned to take on turkey hunting's ultimate challenge. What follows are some tips for those who think they're ready.

KNOW BEFORE YOU GO

Again, your odds for bowhunting success increase substantially if you've had some prior turkey hunting experience. I've guided experienced bowhunters who were first-time turkey hunters, and spoken with many more. They had no idea just how keen-eyed and cautious turkeys can be. After several unsuccessful encounters, they were both awed and disenchanted, and several gave up and switched to shotguns. If you've never hunted turkeys before, I strongly recommend you take a few birds with a gun first. At the very least, spend some time calling and being around birds, and learn as much as you can about general turkey hunting techniques.

Those who have hunted deer already know the challenges of taking game up close and personal. But make no mistake about it: Turkeys and deer are two very different creatures. While deer rely heavily on their acute sense of smell to detect danger, the turkey's number one defense mechanism is its eyesight. As far as shifting position or drawing your bow, deer are a lot more forgiving than turkeys.

CONCEALMENT

Because we bowhunters must draw undetected while in close proximity to a turkey, concealment is especially important. One way to overcome the turkey's keen vision is by using a blind to help conceal your movement. You can fashion one out of natural cover, or add camo material. More recently, I've taken to using a portable pop-up blind, which offers almost total concealment. The down side of any blind, of course, is that it limits mobility. Your chance for a shot depends on luring a bird into one particular area, and they aren't always that accommodating.

Another option is to hunt without a blind, which allows you to reposition, if and when necessary. This requires good camo, extreme patience, composure and a healthy dose of luck. I've found 3-D camo

Portable blinds offer a great option for bowhunters, allowing them to draw undetected when the moment of truth arrives.

Should you decide to hunt without a blind, you can still improve your concealment with a 3-D suit and camo add-ons.

works great at breaking up the human outline and putting birds at ease. You'll still need some cover to hide your movement when you draw. You can crouch or kneel behind brush, or a large-trunked tree. Just remember to allow enough room in front to draw. A small stool will allow you to sit comfortably through those long, agonizing moments waiting for your opportunity. If you hunt without a stool, consider wearing a pair of knee pads. I found I'm more comfortable shooting

Decoys help distract a tom's attention away from you, allowing you an opportunity to draw undetected.

from a kneeling position than sitting, and it offers more mobility. The down side is that kneeling can become a very uncomfortable position if you have to do it for long.

DECOYS

Though, like a blind, they limit mobility, decoys are even more important for the bowhunter. First, they help draw a tom closer. Second, and more importantly, they divert his attention away from you. Third, a tom is much more likely to strut in the presence of a hen decoy.

When a strutting tom turns away, his fanned tail obstructs his rearward vision, offering you an opportunity to draw.

SETUP

The most common setup when hunting from a blind is to place decoys in front, between you and the anticipated direction of the turkey's approach. Most of the camouflage is then also placed in the front. However, as an alternative, some bowhunters will actually place

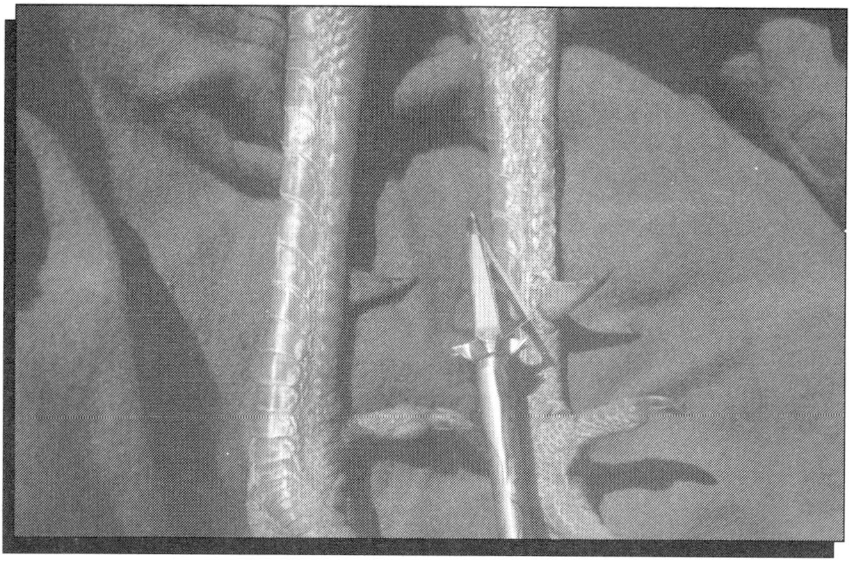

You should affix some sort of stopper device behind your broadheads to prevent complete pass-through shots.

their decoys behind them and slightly off to one side, leaving the back of the blind open. Thus, you are concealed as the turkey approaches. As it draws closer, turn toward the decoys and draw your bow. Once the bird passes by the blind, you have an unobstructed opening to shoot through, and you're already at full draw.

CALLS

Without question, the best call for a bowhunter is a diaphragm. Holding a bow effectively ties up one hand, which precludes most friction calls. However, some of the push-pin type calls come with clips or straps so they can be attached to a gun barrel. It just so happens, the stabilizers on most bows are roughly the same diameter as a gun barrel, and these calls can be attached and used in a similar manner. Another, better option is to pair up and let another person do the calling. It's also more fun to have someone to share the hunt with.

ARCHERY TACKLE

The same archery tackle you use for deer will work for turkeys, with a few minor alterations. Your choice of bow can be somewhat personal; you should shoot a bow that you are comfortable with. Still, compounds have some decided advantages over recurves. One, in particular, is let-off. You have to draw when the bird cannot see you, then hold until you have a clear shot. Those few seconds in between can seem an eternity. Lighter draw weights are also advantageous as they're easier to pull and hold.

Also, unlike hunting large game, you don't want complete pass through. Lighter draw weights help, as does placing some sort of stopper device behind the broadhead. This is totally personal opinion, but I believe fixed broadheads are better than mechanical. The latter are designed to expand on contact with a tough-skinned, large-bodied animal, and could easily pass through a bird without fully expanding.

For sights, I recommend using a single pin set for 15 yards. Too many pins interfere with your sight picture, and may confuse you in the heat of the moment. Remember, your objective is to get the bird to a predetermined area and distance before you shoot. So you shouldn't have to do a lot of range estimating. Just the same, you can hedge your bets by pacing off known distances and using decoys or sticks to mark yardages. Ability varies with the individual archer, but I strongly recommend limiting shots to no more than 15 or 20 yards.

Make sure you check your bow for any shiny or brightly-colored objects. Any thing like a sight screw or a limb bolt that could reflect sunlight should be painted. Also, buy or make arrows with drab-colored fletching, or cover your fletching with a sock. Turkeys will easily pick out bright colors, and red and white are dangerous.

SHOT PLACEMENT

One area in which bowhunting differs radically from gun hunting is shot placement. Crippling loss is always a chief concern, but the probability is higher with archery tackle. Turkeys have a kill zone about the size of a softball. For the gunner, the only reliable target is the head and neck. We bowhunters actually have more options, but our shot must be placed more precisely, because we have only one projectile versus many.

My friend, Jimmy Gaccione, says, "If a guy would put down the gun for one season and resign himself to bowhunting, he would become a much better turkey hunter."

A head/neck shot is very low percentage, but is a hit or miss proposition, the likelihood of wounding being very low. A better option is the body shot. The best angle is broadside, and the point of impact should be right at the butt of the wing. The objective is to hit vital organs, and possibly sever the spine, and this shot offers the highest probability. With a head-on shot, aim for the base of the neck, about where the beard attaches. Caution is advised as the kill zone is smaller, increasing the chances of crippling loss.

A strutting bird offers a more advantageous shot option: the Texas heart shot. When a strutting tom is facing directly away, his keen eyes are hidden by his fanned tail, and he cannot detect our movement. This affords us a chance to draw. That fanned tail also makes for an ideal target, with the bull's eye right at the base of the tail.

Though a lower percentage shot, one final option is "short leg" or thigh, located just aft of the vitals. In order to take off, a bird must first use its powerful legs to vault skyward. Also, they are more likely to run away than fly away. Taking out their "wheels" eliminates both avenues of escape.

RECOVERY

Under the best of circumstances, a shot bird may drop on the spot, or go only a short distance. More often, however, the arrow will pass through, or the bird will shake it, only to run or fly away. This is where attention to detail is critical to recovery. Sometimes you can watch a flying bird until it falls. Mark the spot where you last saw it by picking out some distinct feature, like a tree. Then, take a compass bearing and go directly to that spot. Running birds are harder to follow, and seldom leave a good blood trail. However, a wounded bird will often travel in a straight line. Again, take a bearing on the bird's direction of travel, and begin searching in that direction.

As with wounded deer, it's often better to wait a bit before following up a wounded turkey. If you don't chase them, they'll often crawl into the nearest dense cover they encounter. Don't expect to find the bird lying out in the open, though you may. Look under deadfalls and in brushpiles. Look carefully, as you may only see the tips of their tail feathers protruding from cover. Also, look for feathers, pulled off as the turkey made its way through the underbrush.

If you don't find your bird right away, you may want to enlist help – the more the better. Just as you would for a deer, search the area in a grid pattern, or concentric half-circles, and mark areas as you search to eliminate duplication of effort. How long you search is ultimately up to you. But if you wound a bird, you have an obligation to exhaust all options before giving up. I once wounded a bird in Texas. It took five guys and a dog, and we searched for nearly two hours, but we found the bird.

CONCLUSION

Bowhunting turkeys may not be for everyone, but increasing the level of difficulty in an already challenging sport adds to the to the thrill of the hunt, and your sense of accomplishment. Even if you try it, and ultimately return to the gun, it will also make you a better turkey hunter. My friend, Jim Gaccione, who has taken more than a dozen birds with his bow says, "If a guy would put down the gun for one season and resign himself to bowhunting, he would become a much better turkey hunter. You have to be much more patient. You may have a bird up close for some time before you can shoot, and watching him gives you more insight into things like body language, and how a bird reacts to decoys." All these experiences will add to your knowledge of turkey behavior, and help guide your reactions on future hunts.

thirteen

FALL HUNTING

thirteen

There is such a thing as too close, and that was exactly where I was when the dawn's early light began filtering down through a grove of tall hemlocks. My intent was to set up close to a roost site and intercept the birds as they moved out to feed. I knew about where they roosted, but hadn't made it in the evening before to watch the fly-up, so I just sort of winged it.

I sneaked in well before daybreak, found a good deadfall to hide in, and waited for things to happen. It wasn't long before I heard the first clucks and yelps. Unfortunately, they were coming from almost directly overhead.

The next fifteen or twenty minutes were some of the most exciting in my turkey hunting experience. Turkeys began pitching down on all sides of me: hens and their brood flocks, jakes, even big gangs of gobblers. There had to be close to a hundred birds on the ground, and I had all I could do to keep from moving my head from side to side to see which birds might be coming my way. I finally spied a group of hens that looked like they might be headed in my direction. So I carefully eased myself around into shooting position.

They were slow in coming, though, and meanwhile, a group of gobblers had sneaked in silently from behind. When I heard a twig snap, I craned my eyes around and over my right shoulder just as the flock (there had to have been eight or ten) stepped into bow range. I was about to get busted anyway, so in one fluid motion, I turned and drew my bow, in full view of the birds. I suspect it was because they were so close that they didn't panic and hightail out of there. Instead, their heads went up and they nervously strutted around.

It would have been a chip shot, except for one thing. Just as I came to full draw, my face mask slid up my nose, just enough to obscure my peep sight. There I was, at full draw, 15 yards away from a flock of mature gobblers, and I couldn't shoot. They didn't stick around to give me a second chance. That's fall turkey hunting.

My knowledge of fall turkey hunting is exceptional. By that I mean, most of what I know about turkey hunting I learned from experience, with fall hunting being the notable exception. So much of the information in this chapter comes, not from personal experience, but advice I have gleaned from others.

Fall hunting differs from spring hunting in two ways. First, spring hunting is based on exploiting a gobbler's breeding urge, while fall hunting relies more on the turkey's gregarious nature. Second, spring hunting is for gobblers only, while most fall seasons are for either sex. For these reasons, the methods we use will also differ somewhat. In New England there is a third difference; we can hunt all day. Before we can hunt them though, we've got to find some birds.

FINDING THEM

The first, and most important clue to finding turkeys in the fall is to find a food source. Turkeys are very dependent on, and faithful to, concentrated sources of preferred fall foods. In forested areas, this generally means acorns and beechnuts. In agricultural areas, it may mean waste grain like corn, or green fields with insects. While insects are more important to growing poults in the summer, brood flocks may continue to visit their regular summer haunts through the fall. Transition zones or old fields are also good places to look, as birds will often use them to forage on abundant, soft mast like raspberries, barberries and multiflora rose.

The next key is to locate roost sites. Turkeys don't travel far from reliable food sources in the fall, and you should find roost sites close to food. Keep in mind, however, that a reliable food source could be an oak ridge that stretches a mile or more, and the birds could be anywhere along that ridge. Walking hardwood ridges and looking for sign is a good way to locate both roosting and feeding areas. You tend to find more sign in the fall, because turkeys are concentrated, and there are more of them. As in the spring, look for fresh scratchings in the leaves, and feathers at dusting and roosting areas. Young birds are molting at a rapid rate at this time, and you tend to find more feathers, too.

Listening, particularly at dawn and dusk, is also a good way to locate turkeys close to the roost. Fall turkeys make a lot of noise, especially early in the morning. Hens and poults do a lot of yelping and kee-kee-

While insects are more important to growing poults in the summer, brood flocks may continue to visit their regular summer haunts through the fall.

ing, and jakes especially will sometimes gobble at this time of year. Another, less intensive scouting method involves simply driving around and glassing for birds. Repeated visits will help you pattern birds at a time when they are most patternable. If you're a bowhunter, you can also scout turkeys while you're scouting or hunting deer.

HUNTING THEM

Scattering

A typical fall turkey hunting scenario consists of locating a flock, scattering them, then calling them back together at the hunter's location. It sounds fairly simple, and when it works, it is. Obviously, the first step involves locating a flock, which we've already discussed. The effectiveness of this method then depends on getting a good break. It also depends on the flock composition.

In the fall, turkeys will be segregated into flocks of jakes, toms or hens and their broods. The latter are the easiest to hunt using this method. These brood flocks are very social. Furthermore, the young have probably never been too far away from their mother hen. When they do get separated, they're quite eager to get back together, and they'll usually regroup within the hour. Jakes are less gregarious and

In the fall, birds tend to segregate into flocks of the same sex and age.

dependent on parental guidance, and thus more difficult to call back after the break. Adult toms are the most difficult. Once separated, they will likely get back together, but it may not be for a day or more. So the best odds lie with scattering a brood flock. Some hen flocks may consist mostly or entirely of adult hens. They are less likely to regroup as quickly as brood flocks. You'll need to be more patient and determined in your efforts. You should also use more yelps and fewer kee-kees.

The key to getting a good break is getting as close to the birds as you can, before you rush at them, screaming like a banshee. This helps to scatter them in different directions, which is what you want. If they all scatter in more or less the same direction, they'll likely regroup somewhere away from your position. If you get a bad break, you're probably better off giving up and locating another flock. Subsequent breaks on the same flock are less productive as the birds are now more frightened and close-mouthed. Timing can also be important when using this method. Turkeys are much more inclined to regroup when scattered early in the day.

Assuming you get a good break, move to the position you last saw the flock, set yourself up, wait ten to 15 minutes and begin calling. By then, you may already be hearing the kee-kees or lost hen yelps of lonely birds looking for their running mates. All you have to do is pay attention to what you hear, and mimic it. Be patient, though. It may take birds a half hour to an hour to regroup if you scattered them effectively.

As previously mentioned, the most popular fall calls are the kee-kee and the kee-kee-run. Two other popular fall calls are the assembly yelp and the lost yelp. Both can vary considerably, but a good rule of thumb is: Whatever you hear, you duplicate. You can also call a lot more in the fall, which is just fine with me because I love to call. A non-vocalization that sometimes works alone, or in conjunction with calling, is scratching in the leaves to simulate the sound of feeding turkeys.

Spot-and-stalk

Scattering the flock is by no means the only method for hunting fall turkeys. You can also spot and stalk. You'll cover a lot more ground if you can drive the roads and look for flocks in open fields. Good areas include fields of recently-cut corn, recently-plowed ground or recently-spread manure. Scattering a flock from a field is usually a losing proposition (unless you can team up with another hunter), and you don't actually stalk the birds either—that would be dangerous. Instead, try to determine which direction the flock is headed, then sneak around and set up ahead of them. If they move by you into the woods, then you can revert to scattering. This method is also a good fallback later in the morning, when scattering fails to produce in the early morning.

Positioning

Yet another fall hunting method involves merely setting up along a regular travel route and waiting them out. As already mentioned, turkeys are often very habitual in the fall—roosting in the same trees and moving to and from the same feeding areas on a regular basis. Much as you would in the spring, sneak in before light and set up close to a roost, between the roost and a feeding area (as opposed to directly under the roost). If the birds are following a routine, you may want to go to the extra effort of building a blind at a likely ambush spot. This offers better concealment, which is particularly important for the bowhunter. Several New England states have bow-only fall seasons and this is a great way to bowhunt.

You can sometimes increase the effectiveness of setting up close to a roost by busting the roost just after the birds have flown up, at dusk. The key is to scatter, not scare. The birds will be apart all night, and will be particularly eager to regroup at first light the next morning. This is

A mature tom is the most challenging fall bird to take.

also a good place to end your hunting day. Whether you bust the roost or not, birds may happen by on their way to roost. Just sit and listen. If you hear them flying up, you'll know where to begin the next morning. If you see birds, pay particular attention to the route they take going to the roost, as they'll often follow the reverse route the next morning.

SERENDIPITY

I'd venture to guess that a good many of the birds taken in the fall, particularly by bowhunters, come more or less by serendipity. That is to say, they'll be shot by archers who are hunting deer when either they happen on a flock of birds, or one happens by them. As with deer hunting, a good bit of turkey hunting success depends on being in the right place at the right time. But as someone once said: "Success is where preparation meets opportunity." And the better prepared you are, the more successful you'll be.

The best piece of advice I can offer for those who plan on leaving their opportunities up to the vagaries of fate is: Deer are not turkeys. You're dealing with something that has much keener vision, and is innately predisposed to watching for danger from above. You're also dealing with a creature that has excellent color vision. Turkeys will spot movement or bright objects much quicker than deer will.

Your camouflage must be impeccable, and your movement limited and calculated.

TARGETING TOMS

A mature gobbler is the most difficult turkey to kill in the fall. Add the constraint of archery tackle, and you have a daunting challenge indeed. First, toms just aren't very sociable, and will often be alone or in small bachelor groups. Second, unlike spring gobblers, fall toms have no particular inclination to investigate the calling of hens, or any other turkeys for that matter. When busted, bachelor groups may take hours, or even days, to regroup. This means that patience and scouting are critical.

Hunting a mature tom is, in many ways, like hunting a mature buck outside of the rut. Your best odds for success lie in being where the turkey wants to go anyway. Scout as much as you can, and observe where you see gobblers during various times of day. If you can detect a routine, that will also be helpful. Your calling must also be more conservative, consisting of just a few clucks or yelps. Gobblers do yelp and cluck, though their calls are deeper, coarser and more drawn out than those of hens. If you're trying to call them, yelp or cluck once or twice. Then shut up and wait. If they want to come, they will. If not, additional calling will likely do more harm than good.

EQUIPMENT

In the fall, you'll be using roughly the same turkey hunting equipment as in the spring. Again, you'll need camouflage from head to toe, including gloves, boots and a face mask or face paint. However, you may want to change the particular pattern you wear if your spring camo has a lot of green. By the latter part of October, the leaves have dropped and woods are tinted with drabber grays and browns. Turkeys have excellent color vision, and spring camo pattern with a lot of green may stand out. A better option is a pattern with predominantly browns and grays, or one of the general-purpose patterns like Mossy Oak Break-up, Advantage or Realtree Hardwoods.

BLINDS & DECOYS

You can also use both decoys and blinds in much the same way as you would in the spring. Blinds are especially advantageous for the archer, who must draw while in close proximity to a turkey. The down side is, once you've built your blind, you're committed to that spot. Portable blinds may be a better option, and they run the gamut from a bolt of camo material to a portable pop-up tent. The former is more portable while the latter offers greater concealment. Choose the type that best suits your hunting style. It's also a good idea to carry a set of pruning shears for last-minute trimming.

Decoys don't seem to be as important for fall hunting, but they can help in certain instances, particularly when you're restricted to a blind. In most cases, one decoy is all you'll need. Remember to exercise extreme caution as even hen decoys could also attract the attention of other hunters. Make sure you have a solid back-stop. You may also want to hang an orange ribbon nearby, just to alert other hunters to your presence. Turkeys might see it but they're probably used to seeing surveyor's tape left by loggers, bowhunters or yes, surveyors. More decoys may be more effective, but will be more gear to tote around. In any case, I recommend collapsible decoys for their portability. If you plan on targeting jakes or toms, use similar decoys. Males will be much less likely to join a hen than they would in the spring.

SAFETY/ETHICS/RESPONSIBILITY

Safety should always be foremost on your mind while turkey hunting. You are fully camouflaged, hidden, and imitating the sound of your intended game, as are other hunters in the woods. This increases the potential for an accident. Ethics and responsibility should also be high on your list of considerations. In addition to turkey hunters, you may also be sharing the woods with deer and bird hunters, and knowing proper safety and hunting etiquette can go a long way toward making everyone's hunt safer, and more enjoyable. We'll talk more about this in a later chapter.

FALL HUNTING & TURKEY MANAGEMENT

With the success of turkey relocation efforts in New England, more states are expanding, adding, or considering the addition of fall seasons. The impetus often comes from sportsmen looking for additional hunting opportunities. However, wildlife managers are careful to consider the long term effects of additional hunting effort and its resultant mortality on turkey flocks before implementing such changes. This is especially important as fall seasons typically incorporate either-sex hunting, and hen mortality has a much greater impact on long-term productivity.

Recent studies by the West Virginia Division of Natural Resources and the Virginia Department of Game & Inland Fisheries demonstrated that fall hunting reduces survival and can affect population growth and harvest levels of spring hunting. Principal investigator James Pack and his associates observed that mortality was higher where seasons were longer, and where they coincided with deer firearms seasons. They also found that one way to reduce fall hunting mortality is to move the season away from other seasons with high participation. Another way is to shorten the season.

Several New England states have addressed potential additional mortality associated with fall hunting in part by restricting hunting method. New Hampshire's fall turkey season runs a full three months, but hunting is by archery only. In Vermont, fall hunting by shotgun is permitted in areas where the population can sustain higher harvest levels, but is restricted to archery only in other areas. Maine's two-week fall season is also limited to archery.

It should be noted that healthy turkey populations can tolerate some level of fall hunting with minimal negative impact. In *Turkey Call* magazine, noted turkey biologist Dr. James Earl Kennamer observed that "fall hunting has stood the test of time and can be biologically justified." He cited Pennsylvania and Iowa as states that "have permitted fall hunting for years with correspondingly steady increases in their wild turkey populations where both fall and spring hunting have been allowed."

When setting goals, wildlife managers must look not only at the biological implications, but social issues such as preferences of the resource users, in this case hunters. They must then determine how best to partition that resource to maximize user satisfaction. If the goal is to maximize both the growth rate of a turkey population and spring recreation, results of this study suggest considering only a spring season.

However, if goals include a fall hunt, the Pack study suggests "beginning with a conservative fall season and consider incremented extensions where the effect of each extension is evaluated." The key, according to Pack, is to maintain fall hunting mortality below ten percent of the female segment of the population. This will allow for continued population growth. The more restrictive the seasons, the greater the population growth.

So here we are now, all dressed up with no place to go. We've got a good understanding of the basics of spring and fall hunting, with a few advanced tactics thrown in for those especially difficult birds. Now we need a place to practice what we've learned. In the next section, I'll take you around the six-state region, offering some tips on where you might find some birds.

fourteen

WHERE TO GO: NORTHERN NEW ENGLAND

fourteen

New England turkey hunters have it pretty good in terms of finding both turkeys and places to hunt them. Regardless of where you live in the six-state region, you should be able to find productive hunting grounds close to home. But turkey hunting is addictive. Once hooked, you may feel the desire to travel, and the proximity of the New England states makes out-of-state hunting an attractive option. Many New Englanders live within an hour's drive of at least one other state, and most can reach several states in less than a half-day's drive. You can further maximize your travel time by hunting near the borders; if you add New York to the mix, there are four locations in the region where you can hunt at the corner of three states.

Perhaps the reason more hunters don't take advantage of our region's incredible inter-state and intra-state hunting opportunities is that they don't know where to go. But finding a place to hunt that offers a reasonable chance for success is not all that difficult. You just need to know where to begin looking.

The following two chapters are intended to help you in that regard. They provide state-by-state highlights of where some of the best hunting opportunities exist, based largely on results from recent spring seasons, and the expertise of the individual state's biologists. These chapters are by no means intended as a comprehensive roundup of the best turkey hunting locations in the region. That would take a volume at least as large as this entire book. Instead, they are intended as a general overview, designed to get you pointed in the right direction. This information, and contact information provided for each state, will give you a solid starting point, from which you can fine tune your own search. Besides, finding good hunting grounds is a big part of a successful turkey hunt.

VERMONT

There's no question about it: When it comes to turkey hunting, Vermont is New England's leader. It was the first state to successfully reintroduce birds and hold the first modern spring and fall seasons, and has led the region in turkey population and kill ever since. Much of the success is attributable to dairy farms, despite the fact that roughly 80 percent of the state is dominated by mature forest. According to Vermont's Wild Turkey Management Plan, "Agricultural lands on active farms provide nearly all of the remaining open acreage in the state that is extremely beneficial for wild turkeys." However, the number of small family farms in Vermont has dwindled from nearly 6,000 in 1969 to 1,782 in 1998, with a trend toward larger, more commercial operations in the more fertile valley areas.

That means one way to find high turkey densities is to find farms. Another way is to study harvest records. Records for the past nine years show some consistent trends on where the most birds are taken (Table 1). And not surprisingly, these numbers correspond well with where the farms are.

In terms of spring kill, Rutland County has been Vermont's perennial frontrunner. This includes Wildlife Management Units (WMUs) K1 and K2, most of Unit L and the southern part of Unit I. Of the lot, K2 has been consistently the most productive, with the majority of birds coming from towns west of Route 7, like Clarendon, Danby, Pawlet, Poultney, Tinmouth and West Rutland. This pattern continues south into Unit N, in Bennington County, with most birds also coming from westernmost towns like Dorset, Rupert and Sandgate.

Despite their relatively small size, WMUs F1 and F2, in Addison and southern Chittenden Counties, have also produced a disproportionately high number of birds, compared to units and towns just to the east. Much of the land in all of these highly-productive areas is privately-owned farmland. The best opportunities for public land hunting lie along the western fringes of the Green Mountain National Forest, and in scattered state lands. Top prospects include: Addison, Cornwall, Ferrisburg, Middlebury, Monkton, New Haven and Orwell.

Vermont's other turkey stronghold is WMUs J1 and J2, in Orange County. Success rates have been fairly consistent throughout, though Brookfield, Corinth, Newbury, Randolph and Williamstown are among the top towns. Just to the north, WMUs H1 and H2, in Washington and Caledonia Counties, have produced an increasing number of birds

Table 1. VERMONT SPRING TURKEY HARVEST BY COUNTY, 1994 - 2002

County	1994	1995	1996	1997	1998	1999	2000	2001	2002
Addison	63	134	184	250	391	448	644	630	664
Bennington	96	210	236	263	252	275	330	382	271
Caledonia	12	17	48	61	115	155	236	407	523
Chittenden	14	30	41	90	117	150	216	253	271
Essex	0	0	0	1	2	9	8	20	48
Franklin	0	0	0	0	0	0	0	53	68
Grande Isle	0	0	0	0	21	33	39	40	33
Lamoille	1	0	2	0	3	43	65	69	100
Orange	24	98	134	188	287	419	432	550	573
Orleans	0	0	0	0	0	0	0	104	122
Rutland	100	326	367	518	576	709	756	895	648
Washington	4	19	41	55	119	189	344	361	390
Windham	79	211	129	188	228	300	240	301	273
Windsor	70	160	156	240	332	396	501	561	426
Unknown	0	1	1	4	7	0	7	0	10
TOTAL	463	1206	1339	1858	2450	3126	3818	4626	4420

in recent years, with many of those birds coming from Berlin, Danville, Lyndon and Ryegate. Equally productive have been the belt of Connecticut River Valley towns like Hartland, Rockingham and Weathersfield, in WMUs M2, O2 and Q. Windham and Windsor Counties annually account for a significant percent of the statewide harvest, based largely on those areas.

Another area that has seen a recent increase in harvest rates is Franklin County, Unit B. As recently as 1995, this county wasn't even listed in turkey harvest reports. But in 2001, it accounted for over 100 birds. The state has also been increasing permit numbers and areas open to hunting in Grand Isle County, Unit A. Despite being up in the more remote, and largely forested, Northeast Kingdom region, WMUs D1 and D2, in Orleans and Caledonia Counties, have also produced more birds in recent years.

Hunting is permitted on nearly all state lands, with the exception of some State Parks and most Historic Sites. The Vermont Department of Forests, Parks & Recreation owns 38 state forests encompassing 202,611 acres and 57 state parks encompassing 48,217 acres. The Vermont Atlas & Gazetteer contains a table listing all areas and permitted uses. Forests and parks are also identified on individual maps. You can also get detailed maps and descriptions of individual properties by contacting Vermont State Parks, 103 South Main Street, Waterbury,

Vermont 05671-0601, (802) 241-3655. You can also use the Parks Locator Map on their website at www.vtstateparks.com.

The Vermont Fish & Wildlife Department oversees 85 Wildlife Management Areas encompassing 211,027 acres. These are also listed and depicted in the Vermont Atlas & Gazetteer. Individual maps and descriptions of Vermont's Wildlife Management Areas are available from Vermont Fish & Wildlife Department, 103 South Main Street, Waterbury, VT 05671-0501, (802) 241-3700. These can also be viewed online at www.anr.state.vt.us/wmamaps/index.

Vermont's largest public land holdings are within three districts of the Green Mountain National Forest. Most areas of the forest are also open to hunting under state regulations. Topographic maps and additional information on hunting and other recreational opportunities in the National Forest are available by contacting: Forest Supervisor's Office, 231 North Main Street, Rutland, VT 05701, (802) 747-6700; Manchester Ranger District, RR#1, Box 1940, Routes 11 and 30, Manchester Center, VT 05255, (802) 362-2307; Middlebury Ranger District, RD#4, Box 1260, Route 7, Middlebury, VT 05753; Rochester Ranger District, RD#1, Box 108, Route 100, Rochester, VT 05767, (802) 767-4261.

NEW HAMPSHIRE

Like their Vermont cousins, New Hampshire turkeys are also highly dependent on relatively scarce dairy farms and agricultural land for prime habitat. According to biologist Ted Walski, New Hampshire has fewer than 200 dairy farms in all of its 10 counties. Still, the birds must be doing well in marginal habitat because the statewide population is some 23,000 strong, and continues to grow in number and range beyond anyone's expectations.

According to Walski, Connecticut River Valley WMUs, in Southwestern Cheshire and Sullivan Counties, constitute the state's best turkey range, with WMUs H1, H2 and I2 annually accounting for over 30 percent of the spring take (Table 2). Top towns include Claremont, Cornish, Plainfield and Walpole, in Sullivan County, and Chesterfield, Jaffrey and Westmoreland, in Cheshire County. However, good habitat and turkey numbers exist in most dairy towns bordering the Connecticut River, which contain a mosaic of forest and farms offering the right mix of habitat. Most of the land is private. The one

Table 2. NEW HAMPSHIRE SPRING TURKEY HARVEST BY WMU, 1987 - 2001

WMU	1987	1988	1989	1990	1991	1992	1993	1994	1995	1996	1997	1998	1999	2000	2001
D1	0	0	0	0	0	0	0	0	1	2	4	8	63	84	89
D2	0	0	0	0	0	5	5	0	25	43	51	122	148	218	266
E	0	0	0	0	0	0	0	0	0	1	0	0	0	0	13
F	0	0	0	0	0	0	0	0	0	1	6	19	27	55	61
G	2	1	1	8	4	7	14	15	20	22	48	74	101	141	208
H1	15	28	45	47	69	80	91	67	110	141	145	198	240	303	362
H2	34	36	52	65	71	109	120	134	202	231	243	235	282	324	385
I1	0	0	1	2	2	8	1	11	18	37	31	44	68	91	134
I2	2	1	5	2	14	13	20	25	39	55	51	75	91	139	148
J1	0	0	0	0	0	0	0	0	0	0	0	0	80	75	97
J2	0	3	2	4	4	8	6	6	0	5	13	17	57	101	144
K	0	0	3	3	7	51	31	44	81	101	107	161	154	254	250
L	15	6	13	16	21	29	39	19	25	23	28	23	30	43	59
M	13	14	16	8	10	7	9	13	18	28	30	39	37	55	44
TOTAL	81	89	138	155	202	317	336	334	539	690	757	1015	1378	1883	2260

notable exception being 13,421-acre Pisgah State Park in Hinsdale, Winchester and Chesterfield—one of the largest state land holdings.

Just to the north lies the state's other traditional stronghold, Grafton County. WMUs G and D provide a similarly high proportion of the annual kill, much of that coming from Connecticut Valley towns like Bath, Haverhill, Lebanon and Monroe. Moving east brings you into the foothills of the White Mountain National Forest, which offers plenty of public land with marginal habitat. Again, best odds lie along fores-fringe towns like Rumney and Orange.

Though these areas have been the frontrunners for a while, they've got Hillsborough, Merrimack and Carroll Counties breathing down their neck, and Walski expects that kills in these south-central counties may end up surpassing those of the western and southwestern counties soon. A particularly strong area lies just west of Concord, from New Boston and Goffstown, north and west through Dunbarton, Henniker, Hillsborough and Bradford.

Carroll County towns, particularly those along the southern Maine border, in WMUs J1 and J2, have more recently come on strong too, benefitting from both in-state translocations and dispersal from Maine flocks. In 1999, hunters killed 179 turkeys in Unit J2 and 74 in J1, the first year the latter unit was open to hunting. In 2001, they killed 808 in J2 and 303 in J1.

NEW HAMPSHIRE WMUS

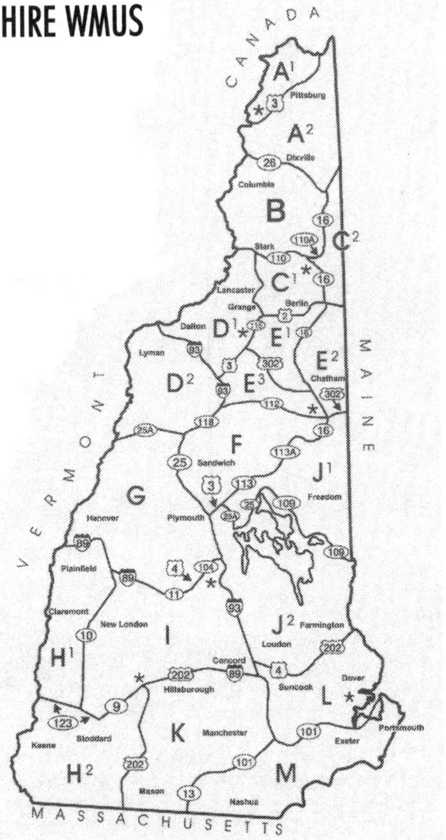

Southeastern Rockingham and Strafford Counties, and northernmost Coos County, represent opposite ends of the spectrum. Turkeys are doing well in the south, where they can find a place to live, but human development continues to crowd them, and those who hunt them, out. Meanwhile, birds have settled into Coos County remarkably well, considering the often severe winter conditions. Some of the county is already open to hunting and Walski hopes to open the remainder soon. It is unlikely turkeys will ever thrive in either region, but there should be enough to keep local hunters happy in Coos County. Hunters in the Southeast may see more need to travel elsewhere in the not-too-distant future.

I had the great fortune to witness friend and fellow outdoor writer Gary Dennis take his first New Hampshire longbeard, a 22-plus-pound limbhanger.

There are four general categories of land ownership in New Hampshire: federal, state, private-industrial and private. According to the Fish & Game Department, "the 'rule of thumb' in New Hampshire is: All state, federal, municipal, county and private land is open to hunting unless it is posted against hunting." However, hunters are reminded that hunting is a privilege granted by the landowner—not a right granted to the hunter.

The White Mountain National Forest comprises over 751,000 acres of federal land. This is the largest single landholding, and represents nearly ten percent of the state's land area. Most of the Forest is open to hunting, except for tourist spots and campgrounds.

Most state lands and state-managed lands are also open to hunting. The Department of Resources & Economic Development owns a total of 201,513 acres in 117 state forests, 41 state parks and 63 other tracts. Most are open to hunting. It also manages three flood control areas totaling 13,446 acres, and conservation easements on thousands of additional acres. The New Hampshire Fish & Game Department owns or has hunting rights to nearly 30,000 acres distributed over nearly 100 Wildlife Management Areas.

Roughly 80 percent of New Hampshire's undeveloped land is privately owned, and most remains open to hunting unless otherwise posted against it. However, the New Hampshire Fish & Game Department highly recommends that each hunter personally contact landowners whenever possible and seek permission to hunt. Timber companies own most of the largest private tracts of land. They and the Fish & Game Department have worked together to provide access to some of the largest private tracts, and most remain open to hunting. Hunters using these lands are asked to respect the landowners by staying off wet or soft roads, giving the right-of-way to logging trucks and equipment, not parking on or blocking any roads or barways and respecting gated or closed roads.

In the early 1990s, New Hampshire invested nearly $47 million, under the Land Conservation Investment Program, to protect more than 100,000 acres of private land from development by buying conservation easements. These easements require that the land remain open to public access, including hunting, in perpetuity. Additionally, many county and municipal lands, such as watershed protection areas, are open to hunting. Conservation easements are depicted in the New Hampshire Atlas & Gazetteer with a light green shade. You should check with local municipalities and county offices for rules regarding hunting on other sites.

For maps and information on the White Mountain National Forest contact: Forest Supervisor, WMNF, USDA-Forest Service, PO Box 638, Laconia, NH, 03247, (603) 524-6450.

MAINE

Due to severe winters, Maine turkeys are also dependent on dairy farms and agricultural areas during the winter. In early spring, however, they disperse over the landscape, and much of southern and central Maine contains a mosaic of small woodlots and fields that turkeys prefer. Populations are thriving in these areas, but are also doing much better than expected in marginal, more forested areas to the north and west.

Region A, in southwestern Maine, is one of the state's two turkey strongholds. Here, regional biologist Phil Bozenhard orchestrated some of the first intra-New England translocations, releasing birds from Vermont and Connecticut into the Mount Agamenticus area of York County in 1977 and 1978. Subsequent stockings occurred throughout the 1980s in various locations in York and Cumberland Counties. The birds took hold and numbers took off, supplemented with additional relocations within the region.

Turkeys are now nearly ubiquitous in the region, though some areas are better than others. Bozenhard observed that, "Wells and Sanford probably have 200 to 300 birds each," and recent harvest data show these two towns as consistent leaders. Bozenhard also identified Gorham, Windham and Standish, in Cumberland County, and Auburn, Lisbon and Poland in Androscoggin County, as good prospects.

I always enjoy guiding my friend, Scott Thompson, from Rhode Island. Our hunts are usually short, and he always buys breakfast.

Region B represents the other, and perhaps greater bastion for turkeys in the Pine Tree State. For hotspots, regional biologist Keel Kemper identified "ground zero" as "Unity, and the surrounding towns of Waldo County: Morrill, Unity, Thorndike, Belfast, etc." As next best, he cited Whitefield, Alna, Pittston and the surrounding towns in Kennebec County. In 2001, hunters took 30 or more birds in Monroe, Albion, Palermo, Jefferson, Pittston and Waldoboro, the latter of which topped the state with 53. This is particularly noteworthy from

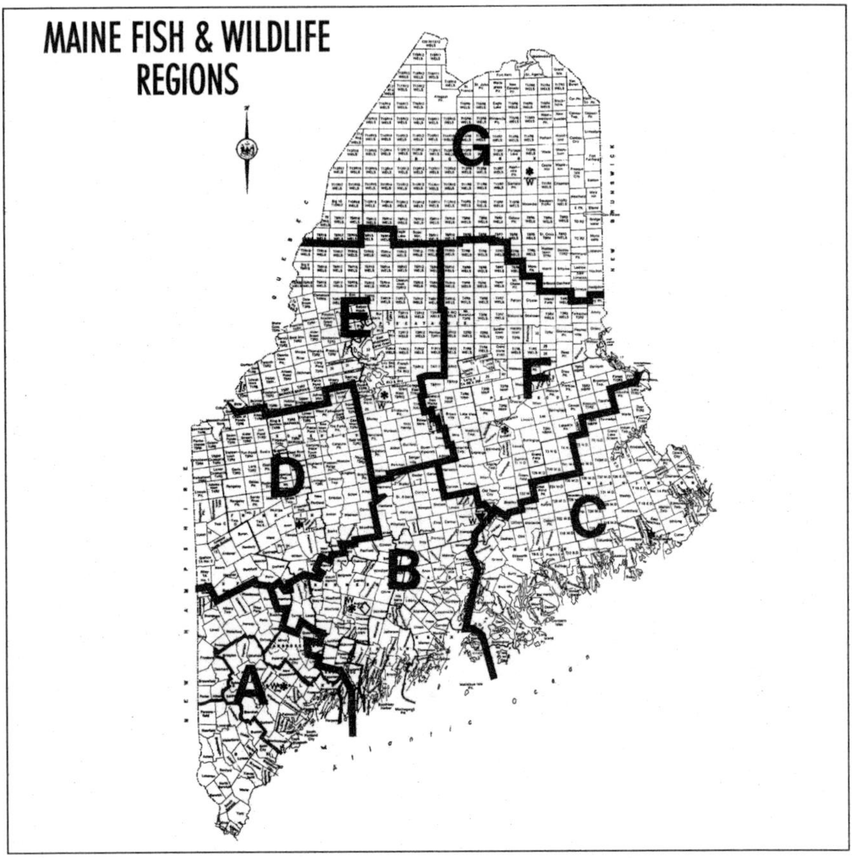

an area where town-wide kills in double-digits are a relatively recent phenomenon.

The current huntable turkey population in Region C is largely the result of three releases in Hancock and Lamoine. Biologists' observations and harvest data suggest good viable populations in Wildlife Management District (WMD) 26 and the western half of WMD 27. There, production is good and birds are staying in release areas. The best hunting opportunities downeast are among established populations in WMD 26 towns along the Penobscot River, and western WMD 27 towns, including: Ellsworth, Trenton, Hancock, Lamoine and Dedham, and up Route 1A toward Brewer. East of there, birds are still at a pioneering level, but the Department continues to release birds along the fringes of established populations.

The Department began releasing birds in Region D in 1997, with 15 birds in Bethel and 11 in Norridgewock. Populations grew so fast in some areas that the Department has already experienced a nuisance problem with over 100 birds at a farm in Bethel. In 1998, they released 16 birds in Madison, and during the winter of 1999-2000, they released 23 birds in Farmington Falls and 44 in Canton.

The birds prospered there as well and towns along the Androscoggin, Sandy and Kennebec Rivers probably have the best potential for this region. That's because this is where you'll find farms, the best habitat, fertile soils and the largest stands of oak. Among the best areas in Region D are the Town of Bethel, along Androscoggin River drainage, the Farmington area along Sandy River and Madison, in WMD 17.

Region E is right on the edge of available turkey habitat. Flocks are small and spread out, and biologists expect that populations will probably always be of that nature–though they've been wrong before. Here, the Towns of Garland, Dexter, Sangerville and Dover-Foxcroft offer the best odds, as that's where the best habitat is.

The progress of restoration efforts in Region F has been surprisingly rapid. Birds were first introduced in the Garland area in 1999. Additional releases occurred in Dover and Bradford the following year, and seemingly overnight, thc populations grew to huntable levels. In 2001, WMD 17 became the first district in Region F open to hunting. Relatively large numbers of birds can be found in the eastern part of WMD 17 in Bradford, Charleston, Atkinson and Milo. WMD 18 was opened for the first time the following year. Here, populations are more sporadic.

According to the Department of Inland Fisheries & Wildlife, roughly 96 percent of Maine's timberland, and virtually all of its working farmland, is in private ownership. Like Vermont and New Hampshire, Maine has a long-standing tradition of implied consent access to private land. Just the same, the Department strongly encourages sportsmen to seek permission.

The largest state land holdings are on the Public Reserved Lands, most of which are outside of the turkey's range. However, MDIF&W manages more than approximately 140 Wildlife Management Areas covering roughly 98,000 acres, all of which are open to hunting, and many of which lie within the WMD's open to turkey hunting.

Maps and descriptions of Maine's Wildlife Management Areas are available from Maine Department of Inland Fisheries & Wildlife, 284 State Street, Augusta, Maine, 04333, (207) 287-5248. To view maps of individual WMAs, visit the Department's homepage at www.mefishwildlife.com.

fifteen

WHERE TO GO: SOUTHERN NEW ENGLNAD

fifteen

Turkey hunting in southern New England has both advantages and disadvantages when compared with turkey hunting in northern New England. Climate and habitat are two of the advantages. Warmer temperatures and less snow mean southern birds are less dependent on dairy farms, have more winter food available to them and can range farther. The southern three states are also relatively less forested. Woodlands often occur in smaller blocks. On a landscape scale, the habit is much more interspersed with fields and farmland, which means the edge habitat that turkeys prefer is much more widespread.

The down side is that the three southern states are more developed. Furthermore, Connecticut and Rhode Island require written permission to hunt on private land, as do many municipalities in Massachusetts. That places greater importance on public lands, which is why they are emphasized more in this chapter. Fortunately, all three states have plenty of public land that is open to hunting. Furthermore, as deer and turkey nuisance complaints continue to increase, more private landowners are becoming amenable to hunting. This chapter provides a run-down of turkey population status and hunting opportunities in the three southern New England states, and contact information to help you refine your search for the best locations.

MASSACHUSETTS

According to MassWildlife's turkey biologist Jim Cardoza, "Turkeys have been successfully introduced everywhere it's practical to have them." Huntable populations now occur in the northeast and southeast portions of the state, and most towns from Route 495, west to the New York border. Within that range, some areas are better than others.

TABLE 3. MASSACHUSETTS TURKEY HARVESTS BY COUNTY, SPRING AND FALL, 1996 - 2002

County	Spr 1996	Fall 1996	Spr 1997	Fall 1997	Spr 1998	Fall 1998	Spr 1999	Fall 1999	Spr 2000	Fall 2000	Spr 2001	Fall 2001	Spr 2002
Barnstable	*	*	*	*	*	*	2	*	15	*	8	*	5
Berkshire	480	69	444	123	458	105	663	89	550	44	565	55	399
Bristol	*	*	*	*	*	*	52	*	45	*	56	*	42
Dukes	*	*	*	*	*	*	*	2	*	2	*	1	*
Essex	*	*	56	*	30	*	58	*	51	*	64	*	65
Franklin	214	28	249	127	265	41	403	97	371	19	360	71	340
Hampden	121	12	131	37	132	28	237	34	196	15	216	29	188
Hampshire	153	15	187	56	181	45	251	53	232	14	231	45	229
Middlesex	1*	*	8	*	10	*	33	*	37	1*	29	*	48
Norfolk	*	*	*	*	*	*	19	*	13	*	17	*	16
Plymouth	*	*	*	*	*	*	99	*	84	*	84	*	91
Worcester	214	*	358	33	359	51	546	29	553	14	533	27	603
TOTAL	1,283	125	1,433	376	1,435	270	2,363	304	2,147	109	2,163	228	2,026

* Closed to turkey hunting.

Berkshire County, particularly the southern Berkshires, where the first reintroductions occurred, has long been a perennial frontrunner in terms of the statewide spring turkey kill, though more recent years have seen a slight decline (Table 3). This area also has some of the state's largest public land holdings. Jug End State Reservation and Management Area in Egremont comprises roughly 1,150 acres. Nearby, Mt. Washington State Forest spans 4,169 acres and Beartown State Forest occupies 10,879 acres in Monterey. That's a lot of public land for such a small state.

The northern Berkshires also offer some fine hunting opportunities, particularly in eastern towns along the Deerfield and Westfield River Valleys. This is where I made some of my first turkey hunting forays. Much of the area is mountainous and forested, but there is ample state land from the corners of Berkshire, Hampshire and Franklin Counties in Hawley, northwest through Savoy, and north to Monroe. Though more developed, there is more open farmland and edge habitat along the Hoosuc River from North Adams south.

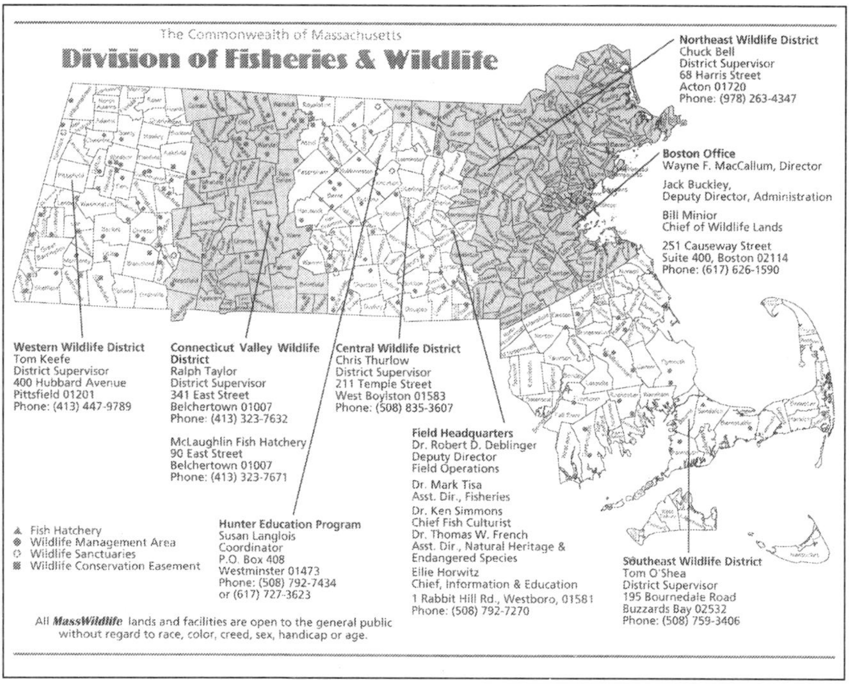

Private land hunting opportunities still exist as well, though some towns, particularly in the southern Berkshires, have "hunting by permission only" ordinances. Posted land is most prevalent in western towns, where the rich and famous dwell. Much of the forested and farm land in the eastern Berkshires is not posted, but asking permission is highly recommended.

To the east lies the Connecticut Valley District, which includes most of Hampden, Hampshire and Franklin Counties. At first glance, the kill totals for each county don't seem so impressive, until you realize that the three counties combined represent an area similar in size to Berkshire County. Of the three, northernmost Franklin County holds a decisive edge in terms of spring kill. It also contains some of the District's larger state lands, which occur in northern towns like Warwick, Northfield, Erving and Wendell. Still, you'll find some of the best turkey habitat, and the most birds in all three counties, in less-developed towns along the Connecticut River valley. Some of Hampshire County's best areas exist in the belt of towns from Amherst, south into Hadley and Easthampton. In southern Hampden County, you can also find good habitat and plenty of birds west of Springfield,

After several frustrating years I finally took my first longbeard in Massachusetts, and a turkey hunter was born.

particularly along the outskirts of Westfield, or east of Springfield, in the largely undeveloped towns around Monson, Brimfield and Wales.

Worcester County has really come on strong in recent years, accounting for an ever-increasing proportion of the statewide turkey harvest. This is no doubt due to both an abundance of public lands, and nearly ideal habitat. Small to medium-sized wildlife management areas are scattered all over north Worcester County in towns like Sterling, Princeton, Hubbardston and Holden. Furthermore, many of the Metropolitan District Commission lands in the Wachusett Reservoir watershed are now open to hunting by permit. Not all are open though, so hunters should check for local regulations and permit information. Habitat conditions are equally good across southern Worcester County, though public land is less abundant.

Kill numbers drop off significantly east of Worcester County, with Plymouth County qualifying as the best of the rest. The largest undeveloped areas and state lands occur in the south: in Plymouth, Carver and Middleborough. Turkeys are also scattered across northeastern Essex County, but hunting is largely limited to smaller wildlife management areas. Most of the land is posted and many towns have ordinances related to hunting or discharge of firearms. Still, if you can find a willing landowner, there are high-density pockets of birds.

The Massachusetts legislature has approved several bond bills for open space acquisition, and legislation filed by the state's sportsmen requires each of them to purchase a five dollar Wildlands Conservation stamp annually for the acquisition of wildlife habitat. The result is more than 600,000 acres of open space (almost 12 percent of the state's total land area) has been protected through purchase or conservation easement. This includes more than 300,00 acres of state forests and parks and over 100,000 acres of wildlife management areas, most of which are open to hunting. The Massachusetts Outdoor Recreation Map provides a complete listing of all state lands and permitted activities.

This publication, as well as maps and descriptions of individual Wildlife Management Areas, are available from MassWildlife, Field Headquarters, Route 135, Westboro, MA 01582, (508) 792-7270, or can be viewed and downloaded from their website at www.state.ma.us/dfwele/dfw. Some properties of the Metropolitan District Commission are also open to hunting. Permit applications and a watershed map showing areas open to hunting can be downloaded from the MDC website at www.state.ma.us/mdc or obtained by contacting: MDC, Division of Watershed Management, Wachusett/Sudbury Section, PO Box 206, Clinton, MA 01510, (978) 365-2372. A map of State Forests and Parks open to hunting is available from the Department of Environmental Management, Division of Forests & Parks, 100 Cambridge Street, Boston, MA 02202.

RHODE ISLAND

Deciding where to hunt in Rhode Island is, in some ways, easy. Because it is so small, and habitat is relatively similar throughout, turkey densities are also similar. According to turkey biologist Brian Tefft, birds now occupy most areas of suitable habitat, though populations are still below carrying capacity in some areas.

The best hunting occurs on private land, which typically accounts for more than 80 percent of the spring kill. If you can gain permission on land that has turkeys, hunt there, wherever it is. If you don't yet have permission, and want to know where to start looking, a quick check of the harvest figures since 1996 shows the Towns of Exeter, Richmond,

Table 4. RHODE ISLAND SPRING TURKEY HARVESTS BY TOWN, 1996-2002.

Town	1986-1996	1996	1997	1998	1999	2000	2001
Burrilville	27	9	15	21	7	16	11
Charlestown	11	4	4	5	7	8	15
Coventry	11	3	4	6	14	12	20
Cranston	1	0	0	2	0	0	8
East Greenwich	1	1	0	0	1	0	2
Exeter	63	11	10	23	27	26	34
Foster	14	8	7	2	8	8	10
Glocester	12	7	4	8	12	8	10
Hopkinton	11	3	5	4	11	8	12
Johnston	0	0	1	2	0	0	3
North Kingstown	0	0	0	2	1	1	4
North Smithfield	2	2	1	1	2	4	3
Richmond	42	14	8	14	22	20	27
South Kingstown	6	1	1	2	11	16	14
Scituate	0	3	6	10	2	3	5
Smithfield	2	2	1	1	6	6	11
Tiverton	0	0	0	0	1	0	1
West Greenwich	1	5	10	15	0	2	6
Westerly	24	0	1	1	3	9	11
Total	228	72	78	119	147	147	207

Burrillville and West Greenwich to be among the top producers, followed by Coventry and Scituate (Table 4).

Public land hunters would also be wise to choose management areas that occur in those towns. Not surprisingly, most do. Largest of the state Wildlife Management Areas, Arcadia encompasses 13,817 acres in Hopkinton, Exeter and Richmond, and annually produces the highest public land kill. Though it is mostly forest, roughly 156 acres are managed in agricultural fields to create food plots and wildlife plantings. Next largest is 8,319-acre Big River WMA in West Greenwich, Exeter, Coventry and East Greenwich.

Burrillville contains parts of three WMAs. Both 1,548-acre Black Hut WMA and 2,049-acre Buck Hill WMA are predominantly forested, though the Division maintains a series of farm fields and food plots at both. George Washington WMA's 3,489 mostly forested acres also lap over into Glocester. Nicholas Farm WMA occupies 1,429 acres in Coventry. Most is forested also, though there are some 40 acres of agricultural fields.

Turkeys have done so well that several states now permit hunters to take multiple birds in the spring.

Larger WMAs tend to receive the most hunting pressure, but also offer more room to roam. Those wishing to avoid hunter interaction need only target some of the smaller sections, or areas away from major roads and access points. There is ample road and trail access throughout most of the areas, though less accessible areas probably experience less hunting pressure.

Maps and descriptions of Rhode Island's Wildlife Management Areas are available from Rhode Island Department of Environmental Management, Division of Fish & Wildlife, or can be viewed online at www.state.ri.us/dem, where you can also view an interactive hunting and fishing map.

CONNECTICUT

One advantage of an established turkey population is there are few surprises.

In general, hunting opportunities are fairly evenly distributed across the Nutmeg State. Though growth rates have slowed, the turkey population continues to grow, as does the spring kill. According to biologist Howard Kilpatrick, "The increasing harvest trends have also been

Some of Connecticut's largest public and best turkey hunting opportunities occur in the northwestern corner of the state.

fairly consistent from town to town," with nearly 150 of Connecticut's 169 towns annually accounting for at least one bird.

However, there are exceptions to this trend. If you look at towns that yield twenty or more birds a year, you can pare the list down to about 35. If you narrow it to towns yielding more than 40 birds, you consistently come up with the same three or four.

One of the state's perennial leaders is Woodstock, in northeastern Connecticut's Zone 5. According to Kilpatrick, Woodstock's kill dropped off to 50 in 2001. It had accounted for 60 or more birds over each of the previous five seasons. Next best in that corner of the state is Pomfret, which is also where you'll find one of the bigger, and more productive state lands: 10,827-acre Natchaug State Forest in Eastford, Pomfret, Chaplin, and Ashford.

Just to the southeast, Sterling has also broken the 60-bird mark. Here you'll find Pachaug State Forest, which spans 9,825 acres in Sterling, Voluntown, Griswold and Plainfield. Other towns in Zone 5 are about equal, though Nipmuck State Forest in Woodstock, Union and Stafford annually yields a disproportionate number of birds.

CONNECTICUT TURKEY ZONE MAP

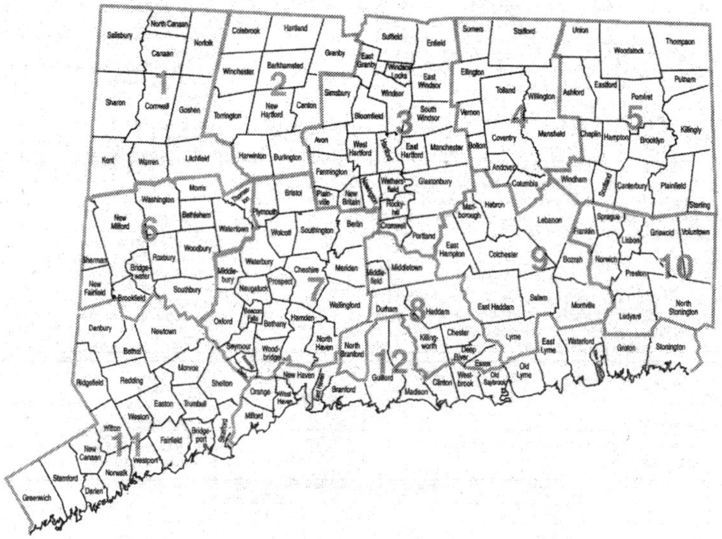

10

Another clear choice for where the best turkey hunting occurs is Zone 1—the northwest corner of the state. This region is the least developed, contains some of the largest public lands, and consistently outscores the rest of the state in terms of spring turkey harvest. Best in the region is the belt of towns running south and west, including Salisbury, Sharon, Cornwall, Goshen and Litchfield. Within these towns you'll find several state lands including Housatonic State Forest, which encompasses over 7,000 acres in several disjunct units spanning multiple towns.

Good habitat and turkey densities persist south into Zone 6, but drop off dramatically once you go south or east of southern Litchfield County. You can, however, find good hunting east into northern Hartford County. Tunxis State Forest in Hartland is a perennial leader, and spans a large area on both sides of Barkhamstead Reservoir.

The state's third stronghold occurs in Zone 9, and includes the towns of Lebanon, Colchester, East Haddam and Lyme, in New London County. Much of the land is private, with Salmon River and Nehantic State Forests being notable exceptions. Undeveloped towns along the fringes of these three hotspots are certainly worth investigating too.

And like Rhode Island, if you can gain permission to private land that holds turkeys, hunt there.

Maps of Connecticut's Wildlife Management Areas are available from Connecticut Department of Environmental Protection, 79 Elm Street, Hartford, CT 06106-5127, (860) 424-355, or visit them on the web at www.dep.state.ct.us.

The DeLorme Mapping Company now has an Atlas and Gazetteer for every New England state. These books are invaluable for finding your way around. In addition to containing detailed road maps that also show topography, they contain a wealth of information on local facilities and attractions. Contact DeLorme Mapping at 2 DeLorme Drive, Yarmouth, Maine 04096, (207) 846-7000, or visit their website: www.delorme.com.

MapTech's Terrain Navigator series contains a complete set of U.S.G.S. topographical maps on CD-rom. Contact: Maptech, Inc., 10 Industrial Way, Amesbury, MA 01913, (978) 792-1000, or at www.maptech.com.

sixteen

TURKEY HUNTING ETIQUETTE & SAFETY

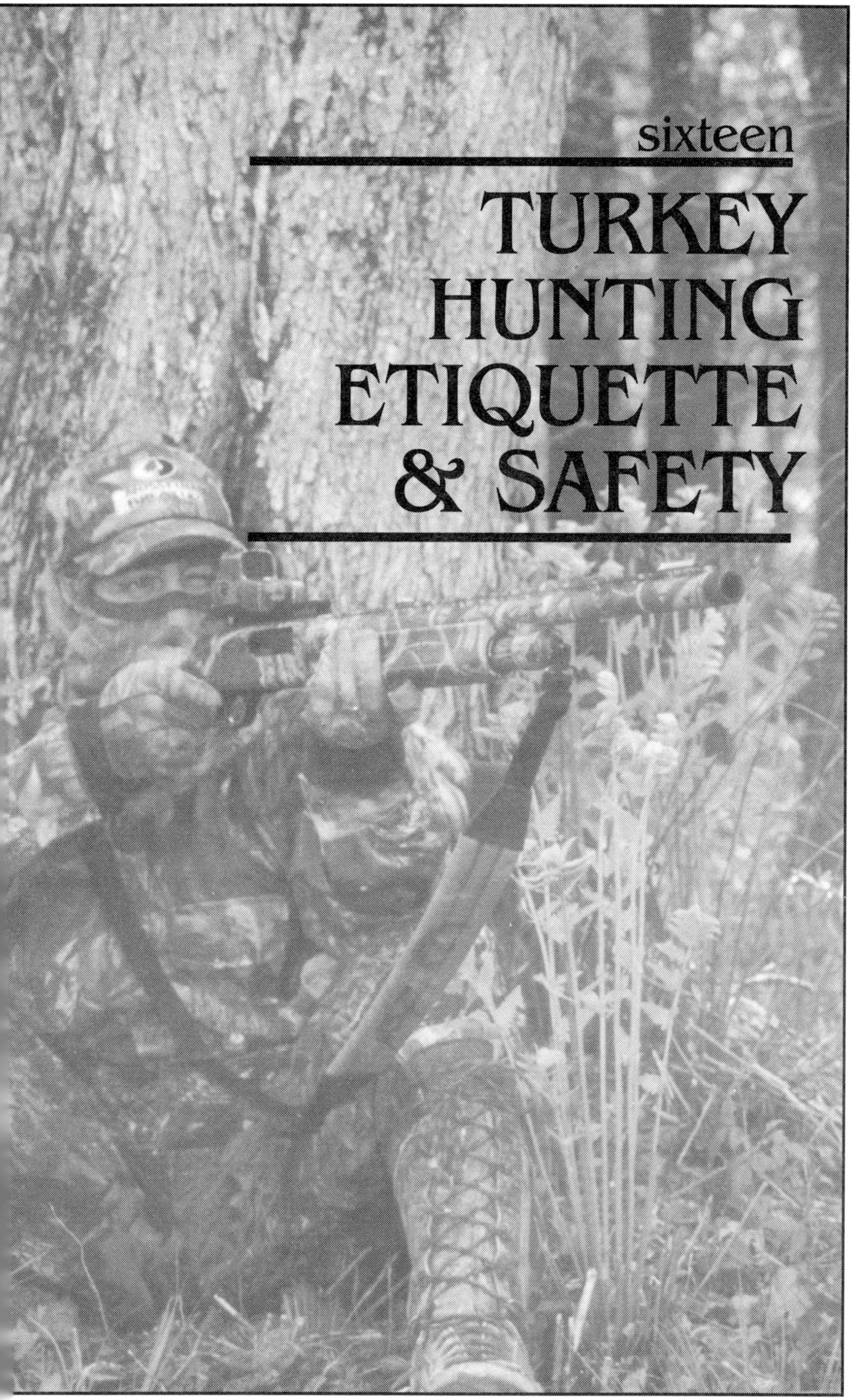

sixteen

The predawn sky was still filled with stars as my client and I slipped along the edge of a large field. Our destination was the high-point in the field, where a small finger of woods jutted out. I figured this would give us, and our decoys, maximum visibility; we'd see anything coming, and anything coming would see our decoys. We were also about as close as I wanted to get to a pair of gobblers I'd roosted the evening before. I set out my decoys and built a makeshift blind along the field edge.

It was just about the time the first rosy rays of light appeared in the eastern sky when the gobblers announced their presence. I still couldn't make out my hunter's face in the darkness, but I noticed his breathing had suddenly become much heavier. "Here we go," I whispered, as I began a few soft tree yelps. I didn't want the birds to come down, not just yet. So I held off calling until it got lighter.

It was several minutes after the start of legal shooting hours when I chimed in with some soft yelps and clucks, and I was just about to do a fly-down cackle when I saw another hunter walking down an adjacent field, directly toward us. It was now light enough that he should have been able to see our decoys, especially as they were on the crown of a hill. And unless he was stone deaf, he had to hear my calling. I shined my flashlight in his direction and gave several loud yelps, more for the interloper than the turkeys. Still, on he came.

For a moment, he disappeared into a windrow that separated our field from his. Then, he reappeared on our side, stepped into the open and began setting out his decoys, no more than 150 yards from us, and directly in line with our decoys! I was awestruck by his audacity. I shined my light again, waved my hand and even whistled, but the other hunter simply ignored us, stepped back into the brush and sat down.

The gobbling had stopped now, which had me even more concerned. I wasn't sure if it was because he'd spooked them, which would have been bad enough, or because the birds had flown down and were coming in, which could have been potentially dangerous, if they somehow managed to get between us and the other hunter.

In retrospect, I probably should have left right then. But I had a paying customer with me, had roosted the birds the previous evening and gotten in and set up well before daylight. These were *my* birds. I decided to stay put a while, hoping the birds might sneak in silently from behind, but I was extremely uncomfortable with the situation. After about thirty minutes, the interloper stepped back out into the field, picked up his decoys, and went back out the way he'd come in. His morning was over. Ours wasn't, but he'd ruined the best part of it.

Turkey hunting can be one of the most exciting and enjoyable shooting sports, when done properly. Unfortunately, it can also be one of the most frustrating and potentially dangerous when hunters fail to follow a few common sense guidelines. Safety should always be foremost in the mind of every turkey hunter. Ethics and consideration for other hunters should be a close second. Dozens of new hunters enter the sport every year, and their unfamiliarity with it can sometimes lead a novice unwittingly into an unsafe situation, or result in unintentional interference. That's why knowing proper safety and turkey hunting etiquette can go a long way toward making everyone's hunt safer and more enjoyable.

The interloper in the above story violated one of the cardinal rules of turkey hunting: Never, ever move in on a bird that someone else is calling. It is both unethical and unsafe. At best, you might screw up their hunt. At worst, someone could get shot. If you hear a gobbling tom, especially in a heavily-hunted area, stop some distance away and listen, to be sure you're alone. If you hear another hunter calling, or if you see decoys, leave. If not, be patient and careful. Don't charge in assuming there's no one else there. Another hunter could be working the bird with soft, well-spaced calls.

If you don't see or hear any sign of another hunter, you should still be cautious, and don't try to get too close. Ninety-nine out of 100 times, a sharp-eyed (and sharp-eared) gobbler will see or hear you long before you see him. Also, a gobbler will often make his final approach to a hunter silently. That hunter, who may have stopped calling, is looking for movement—any movement—and listening for quiet footsteps. While it should never happen, in thick brush you could be mistaken for the turkey you're trying to sneak up on.

In any event, you should never try to stalk a turkey. Two Maine hunters learned that lesson the hard way in 2002. Spotting two decoys in a field, which they presumed to be real turkeys, the pair made a long stalk. Meanwhile, two other hunters were sitting just inside the field edge, calling. Hearing something approaching from the rear, one peered around from behind the tree he was sitting against. Seeing the movement, one of the stalkers presumed it to be a turkey. He fired, hitting the seated hunter in the head and shoulder. The wounded hunter survived, but suffered permanent injuries.

That incident was preventable. There were a number of reasons it occurred, chiefly because a hunter was trying to stalk a turkey. He was a first-time turkey hunter, and perhaps didn't know he was doing anything wrong. But that's a spurious excuse. If he had applied a little common sense, and bothered to read the safety information the state of Maine distributes to every turkey hunter, he should have known better. Perhaps he did, but the pressure to succeed was too much.

That brings up another important point. No turkey is worth risking your safety, or that of another hunter. We sometimes put too much pressure on ourselves to succeed, failing to remember that not all hunts need to end with a bagged bird in order to be successful. I've learned some of my most valuable lessons through failed hunts. Even if you don't bag your bird this year, there's always next year. On the other hand, an accident could mean an end to your turkey hunting career or even your life.

Another reason turkey hunting can be potentially dangerous is that we are trying to imitate the sound of our quarry. Granted, in the spring we're hunting gobblers and imitating hens, but some hunters are drawn to the sound of hens, perhaps hoping there are gobblers with them. If you hear hen calls, always assume it's another hunter first, and shy away from them, or at least move no closer. Some of the most authentic calling I've ever heard in the woods turned out to be another hunter, while some of the worst turned out to be the genuine article.

Making other hunters aware of your presence is also good practice. How you should do this will vary with the situation. Often, turkey hunters will move and call, move and call. If you hear someone doing this, give a few loud yelps, just to let them know you're there. If they hear this, they should move away. If not, try using a non-turkey call like a high-pitched dog whistle, or a crow or woodpecker call. This will alert them to your presence without unnecessarily alarming any nearby turkeys. If that doesn't work, you may have to resort to unnatural sounds.

It's always better to ruin a hunt than to ruin a life. In the unlikely event that someone has come within shotgun range and is still unaware of your presence, don't make any sudden movements or loud noises. Try to get their attention first by whistling, or talking in a low tone. Increase the volume of your voice gradually until you are heard, and noticed. Never assume they've recognized you until you are certain.

One of my most sobering experiences came as I was trolling along a woods road one morning, walking and calling. I came around a bend and caught sight of a reddish object that looked exactly like the head and neck of gobbler, less than thirty yards away. I froze, and stared for several seconds while my mind sorted out the details of what I was looking at. Eventually I realized it was the sun shining on the face of another hunter. He never moved or made a sound until I held up a shaky hand to acknowledge his presence. Perhaps he felt safe because my gun was slung over my shoulder, which is how I always carry it when walking. I shudder to think of what might have happened had another, less responsible or less experienced hunter been in my place.

When traveling through the woods yourself, it's a good idea to display some orange. This is not only a matter of safety for you, but consideration for fellow hunters. Some hunters will even tie an orange ribbon above their head to alert others to their presence. There's a chance it may spook a gobbler, but with all the survey flagging in the woods these days, most birds are used to it.

One of the best ways to avoid interference or potential problems is to avoid crowded areas. Some places, usually those with the most visible birds, just seem to draw the crowds. And the more turkey hunters you put in an area, the greater the chance for problems, and the less your odds for success. Sure, maybe there are lots of birds there, but more than likely you'll end up getting frustrated. Just as you get set up and start to call, some nimrod bumbles in and blows it for you (remember the opening story from this chapter?). Besides, resident birds in pressured areas become call shy quickly, making them harder to kill.

If you arrive at your favorite spot and there is already a vehicle there, move on. Just as with duck blinds and deer stands, turkey hunting etiquette says that the spot goes to the first person there. Besides, if you've done your homework, you should have several "Plan Bs" in case someone beat you to your honey hole. Being a guide, I'm especially sensitive to this, and always yield when someone gets there ahead of me, which doesn't happen very often.

Keep an eye out for decoys too, and react to them the same way you do to "Posted" signs—keep away, far away. This is especially important around fields, as turkeys can see a long way in the open, and someone could be working a distant bird that you don't see. When hunting around fields it's also a good idea to approach slowly, in case there are birds in the open. I was once calling a tom in a field in western Massachusetts. He was coming straight to me, like he was on a string. Suddenly, he stopped, putted and bolted into the woods. A few minutes later another hunter came along, head down, casually walking up the middle of the field.

ASK FIRST

Connecticut and Rhode Island are currently the only states that require written permission to hunt on private land, though municipalities in some other states also have this requirement. In the remaining states, access is implicit on unposted property. However, hunters should be reminded that trespassing on private land for purposes of hunting is a privilege, not a right, and they should always attempt to ask first.

Once you have gained permission, behave yourself. Treat the land, landowner and other hunters with respect. And just because you have exclusive rights to hunt a particular piece of property, don't assume you're the only one there. As humans continue to increase in number, and sprawl out into the suburbs and rural areas, they bring with them posted signs and an urban predisposition against hunters. Furthermore, one irresponsible act on the part of a single hunter can do irreparable damage to the image of all hunters.

Turkey hunting can be a potentially dangerous sport, when those who participate don't follow the rules. The most common cause of accidents is hunters being mistaken for game. Again, safety should be your foremost consideration at all times. To ensure a safer and more enjoyable hunt for you, and those sharing the woods with you, The National Wild Turkey Federation recommends you always observe the following few safety rules:

• **Never wear the colors red, white or blue.** These are the gobbler's head colors, often used by hunters to distinguish legal game, and wearing them could draw fire.

• **Always select a calling position that provides a background at least as wide as your shoulders.** This will protect your rear, and help conceal movement from a turkey.

• **Always select a calling position that provides good visibility in a 180-degree field of view.** This will allow you to see other hunters and them to see you.

• **Never make sudden movements when calling**. Not only could this alert a turkey to your presence, it could result in another hunter mistaking you for a bird.

• **Always assume that sounds you hear may be made by another hunter.** Some of the best callers in the woods are not turkeys, and some of the worst are. Take nothing for granted and be certain of your target before you shoot.

• **Always identify your target before you shoot.** First, be certain it is a turkey. Then, make sure it is a legal bird. Most states limit you to a bearded bird, some limit you to a male (bearded hens do occur) and others prohibit shooting jakes (young males which usually sport a three to five-inch beard).

•**Never stalk a wild turkey.** It is dangerous, and could put you in the line of fire of another, unseen hunter. Besides, your odds of doing so successfully are astronomically low.

•**Never use a gobble call to call in birds.** You are much more likely to call in other hunters.

•**Never carry a bird out of the woods exposed.** Carry it in a vest, or bag specifically designed fore the job.

Go out there, enjoy, be considerate and above all else, hunt safely.

seventeen

SCORING YOUR TURKEY

seventeen

Tell someone from New England that you shot a big buck and I'll bet their first question will either be: "What did it weigh?" or "What did it score?" Tell them you shot a big turkey, and it's much more likely they'll ask about the weight. A lot of turkey hunters don't even know turkeys can be scored, and of those that do, many probably don't know how to do it. Just as the Boone & Crockett and Pope & Young Clubs maintain records of, and have a scoring system for, trophy big game animals, The National Wild Turkey Federation maintains official records of wild turkeys taken by fair chase methods anywhere in the world. To do so, they have developed a fairly simple scoring system, which has also been adopted by many states and other private trophy organizations. Their system consists of a combination of three measurements: live weight, beard length and spur length, which are recorded as follows.

WEIGHT

Turkeys should be weighed to the nearest ounce on a certified scale, official scale of a government wildlife agency, or on an accurate scale by a licensed guide or outfitter. While live weight is not a requirement, it is the recommended measurement as it is heavier than dressed weight, and thus will yield a higher score.

BEARD LENGTH

The beard is measured from the center point where it protrudes from the skin to the end of the longest bristle. Bristle length tends to be fairly uniform on an individual beard but you may have one or two that are noticeably longer. Pay particular attention to these as they will boost your score.

The beard is measured from the center point where it protrudes from the skin to the end of the longest bristle. Bristle length tends to be fairly uniform on an individual beard, but you may have one or two that are noticeably longer. Pay particular attention to these as they will boost your score.

Spur Length

Spur length is measured along its outside edge, from that point where it protrudes from the scaled leg skin to the tip of the spur.

Both of the latter two measurements are made to the nearest one-sixteenth of an inch. Unlike antlers, which require a drying period, beards and spurs can and should be measured as soon as possible, as drying will detract from the score. They can also be measured after the legs and beard have been removed from the bird, but this also usually results in a lower score.

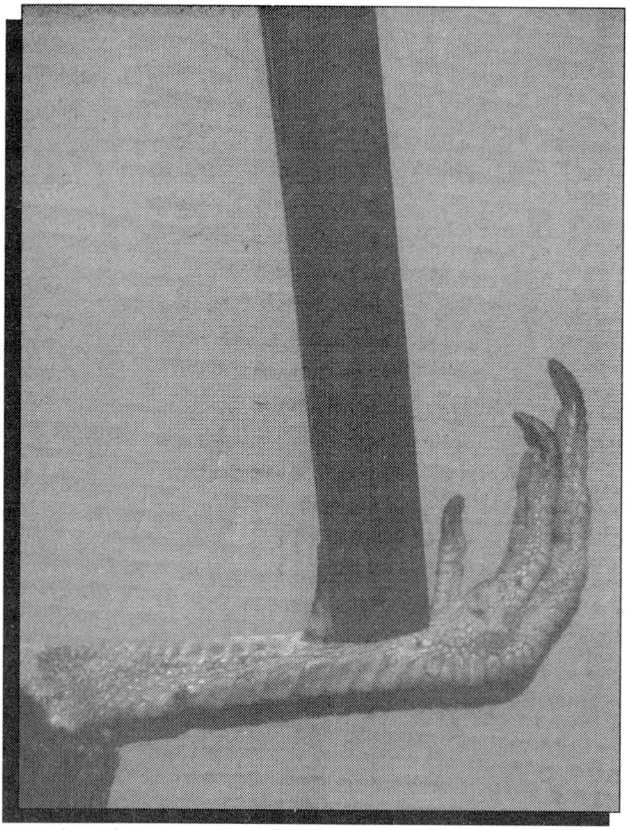

Spur length is measured along its outside edge, from that point where it protrudes from the scale leg skin to the tip of the spur.

These measurements are converted to decimals, then combined using the following formula to derive a total score. Score = (weight) + (2 x beard length) + (10 x (right spur length + left spur length)). Example: (21.4 pounds) + (10.5 x 2) + ((10 x 1.25) + (10 x 1.25)) = 67.4.

Occasionally, a bird will have more than one beard. Such toms are categorized as non-typical. In this case, the combined length of all beards is summed, multiplied by two, then added to the weight and spur-length calculations.

The NWTF's records are intended not as a ranking system, but a permanent record of all birds harvested; there are no minimum size qualifications for entry. Just the same, every year the Federation publishes the top twenty entries to date in each of the categories they recognize, which include Eastern, Florida (Osceola), Rio Grande Merriam's and Gould's.

The current world-record turkey is an Eastern, taken in Kentucky in 1996 by Allen Vanderpool. The bird sported an 11-inch beard and spurs of $1^{1/2}$ inches, but weighed and incredible 34 pounds, also making it the heaviest bird on record. According to NWTF records, the longest recorded spurs are $2^{1/4}$ inches, and the longest beard is $18^{1/4}$ inches. Official registration forms are available from the NWTF. All entries must be signed, witnessed and mailed to the National Wild Turkey Federation, PO Box 530, Edgefield, SC 29824-0530.

Several New England states also have trophy clubs. The Maine state chapter of the National Wild Turkey Federation has established the Longbeard Society, which recognizes hunters who have taken trophy wild turkeys. To qualify, a turkey must have been legally taken in Maine, and have a minimum beard length of seven inches.

While they do note base Longbeard Society qualification on weight or spur length, they do require that you record this information on your registration form. Your turkey must be weighed to the nearest ounce on scales inspected and certified as accurate for trade by the U.S. Department of Agriculture, or on the scales at a check station provided by the Maine Department of Inland Fisheries & Wildlife.

Beard and spur length measurements must be made in the same manner described above. Turkeys weighing 21 pounds or more, having beards of ten inches or longer, or having spurs of $1^{1/4}$ inch or longer must be measured by an official Maine state chapter scorer. To locate one, contact the NWTF's Maine chapter at the address listed in Appendix 1.

In order to register your trophy and join the Longbeard Society, you must be a current member of the National Wild Turkey Federation. The Maine state chapter will issue a Longbeard Society patch to each member who registers a qualifying turkey and pays a $5 registration fee to help cover the program's expenses.

The Vermont Big Game Awards Program also recognizes turkeys by NWTF score. Trophy turkey entry cards are available at each wild turkey reporting station—presumably to be used and filled out while reporting a harvested bird. Birds scoring over 63 points are listed in the annual results, and there is a September 1 deadline for submission. Contact the address listed in Appendix 1 for more information.

The other New England states do not currently have their own trophy recognition programs. However, birds taken from any state are eligible for the NWTF's National records program.

FIELD-JUDGING TROPHY TOMS

Black bear, sheep and goats are considered to be among the most difficult big game animals to field judge. Wild turkeys could, and probably should, be included in that list, but they aren't for several reasons. First, many hunters don't consider them a big game species. Second, fewer participants are actively seeking out trophy birds. Neither will be the case for long. As the wild turkey closes in on the white-tailed deer as North America's most popular big game animal, more turkey hunting enthusiasts are holding out for trophy toms. In order to do so, you need to know when to pass and when to shoot.

As mentioned above, a turkey's score is determined by three measurements: weight, beard length and spur length. These three characteristics, particularly the latter two, generally increase with age. So the older individuals will generally score the highest. None of the characteristics are easy to judge in the field, but there are a few helpful tips.

Weight

Of the three measurements, weight can be the most difficult to field-judge. Experienced hunters can sometimes tell a big bird from an average-sized one. Having other toms around for comparison is also helpful as you can compare relative sizes. Hens provide a less reliable comparison as toms are considerably larger than hens.

Trophy hunters should also bear in mind that heaviest birds are not necessarily the oldest, or the highest-scoring. As with whitetails, the oldest males dominate, and do most of the breeding. Preoccupied with courtship and fending off rivals, these boss toms lose weight, particularly toward the end of the season, and are often lighter than their younger rivals. They'll still out-score a younger, heavier bird. However, some hunters may prefer to judge their trophy by weight rather than score.

Beards

Beard length is also best judged as a relative comparison, but can be judged on individual birds. Two-year-old birds generally have beards of eight or nine inches, while older, trophy-class toms typically have beards of at least ten inches. When viewed from the side, the beard of an upright, two-year-old tom will hang down just about even with its belly. If the beard dangles noticeably lower than the belly in profile view, it's a good indication of a trophy. If the tip touches the ground when the bird is in full strut, shoot!

In a flock containing multiple toms, the strutting bird is most often the older and more dominant bird.

Spurs

Like the horns of a goat or sheep, a turkey's spurs continue to grow longer throughout its life. The older the bird, the longer its spurs. And because the scoring formula multiplies them each by ten, spur length is what really boosts a trophy's score. One-inch spurs usually indicate a three-year-old and any bird with spurs of $1^{1/4}$-inches or more is at least a four-year-old. Of course, these are generalities and can vary considerably.

It may be difficult, if not impossible, to tell the difference between 1-inch and 1 1/4-inch spurs in the field, which makes them a less reliable field indicator. You can use a couple of clues, however. As spurs become longer, they tend to become narrower, and more pointed toward the tip. They also begin to curve upward. You can actually hang a very old bird on a horizontal branch by its spurs; thus the term "limb-hanger." Binoculars are helpful in making out these characteristics the field, if you have the luxury of being able to glass a bird before you must commit.

Behavior

A tom's behavior can also help in identifying it as a trophy. As mentioned above, the older birds are often the dominant ones, and do most of the breeding. In a mixed flock of toms and hens, the boss tom will most often be the one doing the strutting. He'll also be bullying the other toms, and driving them away from the hens. The boss gobbler will also be the wariest, having survived several seasons, and whether he scores high or not, any such bird is a trophy. Also, while killing a bird that scores high is certainly an accomplishment to be proud of, it is more often the circumstances that go into taking it, not the size of the bird, that defines it as a trophy.

eighteen

PRESERVING YOUR TROPHY

eighteen

Regardless of weight, or beard or spur length, I consider any wild turkey taken by legal and ethical means to be a trophy. It could be a big, long-spurred limbhanger that meets the conventional definition, or it could be a smaller bird that offered a particularly challenging hunt. Maybe it's your first wild turkey, or your first with a bow. Regardless, each and every turkey you kill should be fully appreciated, and treated with the respect worthy of such a magnificent bird, whether it ultimately ends up in your trophy room, your dining room, or both. In this chapter are some ideas on how to handle your bird for whatever your intended purpose is.

THE TROPHY ROOM

Even before you kill your bird, you should have an idea whether you intend to save some or all of the turkey for mounting purposes. You have several options. One is a full mount. In this case, you'll need to preserve the turkey intact, and in the best condition possible. Try to wipe or rinse off any blood immediately, and avoid ruffling the feathers, particularly those of the fan. You may want to carry a few cotton balls, which you can stuff in the bird's mouth to absorb any blood.

You may also want to carry a two-foot length of nylon stocking, the upper or thigh section. Tie a knot in one end, then slide the turkey, head first, into the stocking. This will hold the feathers tight against the body and keep them in place. Try to keep the bird cool until you get it home. Then, wrap it carefully first in newspaper, then in a plastic garbage bag, and put it in the freezer. Or, bring it directly to your taxidermist.

You also have several options for a partial mount. A head and fan mount is attractive, economical and takes up a bit less space in the trophy room. If that is your intention, treat the bird in the same manner you would for a full mount.

Skin Mount

Another option is a full skin mount. You can take the bird to your taxidermist, or you can do it yourself. To prepare a skin mount, begin by making an incision in the skin, from the vent up the center of the breast to the base of the neck, where the feathers end, and skin around the base of the neck. Next, carefully skin the entire bird, without further incisions if possible. You can remove the wings by cutting at the shoulder joint, then cutting the skin around the base of each. You may want to sew these two incisions closed so the holes don't show. If you decide to leave the wings in place, you should slit open the skin on the underside and remove any flesh or fat.

Remove any remaining flesh or fat from the skin, too. Then, rub a mixture of salt and borax into the skin. The salt will help to dry out any residual fat or tissue and the borax will help preserve the skin and prevent insect infestation. Turn it over, spread it out and tack it to a board to dry. That's about it. When the skin has dried, you can trim around the edges to neaten them up. You can also sew the skin onto a piece of felt, much the same as a bear skin rug.

Fan Mount

One of the more popular ways to display a turkey is with the fan and beard mounted on a plaque. Again, you can do it yourself or take it to a taxidermist. It is a fairly easy process if you choose the former. First, remove the beard by cutting it away from the breast. Be sure to leave enough flesh at the base to keep the bristles intact. Moisten the base and dip it in a solution of salt and borax. Then set it in a well-ventilated area to dry.

Next comes the tail. Cut the tail off at its base, leaving enough flesh and bone so the fan remains intact. Turn the tail over. On the back or bottom side, carefully begin filleting the flesh away by guiding your knife blade along the shafts of the large tail feathers. You'll soon encounter a bone at the center of the fan base. Leave this intact, for now.

Field Dressing A Wild Turkey

Note: On a bird you suspect may weigh in excess of 20 lbs., you will want to weigh the bird whole, **on certified scales.**

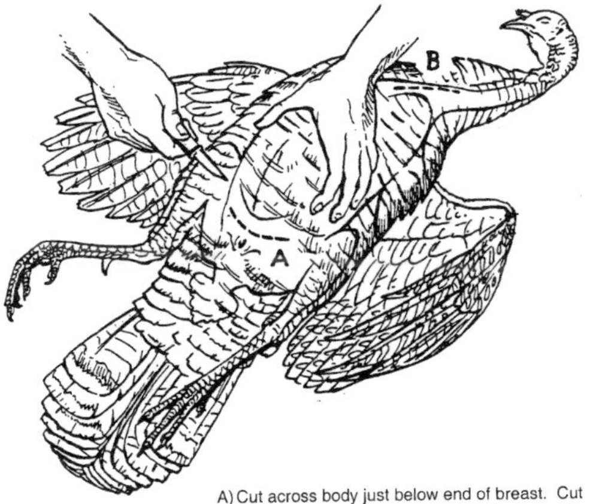

A) Cut across body just below end of breast. Cut around vent and pull out contents of body cavity.

B) Cut along base of neck and pull out crop.

REPRINTED BY PERMISSION OF MAINE DEPARTMENT OF INLAND FISHERIES & WILDLIFE.

Turn the tail over, and do the same thing on the top. You may want to leave several layers or tracts of secondary tail coverts, the smaller tail feathers, in place. If you look carefully, you will find a small fleshy appendage with several short, waxy feathers at the end. This is the tip of the oil gland. I usually begin filleting just above this and down, removing the gland and all flesh and feathers below it, but save the feathers for mounting later. Now, with a pair of diagonal cutters, remove the bone in the center of the tail base. This should leave you with a full, intact fan. Carefully remove any remaining flesh and fat, then cover the base of the quills with salt and borax. Next, spread the fan out, lay it flat and fasten it to a board so that it will dry in this position. You may also want to place something on top of it so it remains flat.

Once the fan has fully dried, you can replace some of the shorter feathers, fastening them in place with hot glue. You can purchase game bird fan mount plaques that come with slots for the fan and beard at most outdoor retailers, or, you can make your own. Hot-glue the beard in the bottom slot and the fan in the top slot, hang it on the wall and enjoy it.

Beards and Spurs

Some hunters prefer to save only the beards and spurs, and there are several things you can do with them. When dressing your bird, cut off the legs, just below where the feathers end, and set them aside to dry. After they have dried sufficiently, remove the spur by cutting across the leg, through the bone above and below the spur, leaving a short length of leg bone with the spur still attached. With a Q-tip, clean the marrow from inside the leg bone. You can either leave the scaly skin attached, or peel it off, depending on the desired look. Let them dry, then string the spurs on a piece of rawhide, to make a necklace or hat band.

After removing the beard and drying it as described above, you can display it in one of several ways. One way to attractively display your beard is in the brass base of a shot shell. First, remove the plastic hull of the shell and the primer from the brass. Next, hot-glue a small loop of rawhide or cord to the base of the beard. Then, pull this loop through the primer hole, pulling the base of the beard up into the brass. Glue in place and hang on the wall. You can also hang one or more beards on a separate plaque, which you can buy or make.

THE DINING ROOM

The wild turkey is arguably our most delicious gamebird. I've eaten just about everything you can legally kill in New England, and have yet to find any feathered game that is better. The quality of the meat will depend on several things, especially how your care for the bird after killing it. What steps you take will depend to some extent on how long it takes to go from the field to the frying pan.

Your first priority should be cooling the bird down and keeping it cool, especially if you plan on weighing it round. While it is not a requirement, most hunters prefer to bring their birds to the check station un-gutted, as this renders a higher weight. If it's cool out, you can bring it to the check station, and then home, without too much worry. If it's warm, put the bird in a cooler, or wrap it in a coat with a bag of ice until you get home.

In the field, or at home, you have two basic options with regard to how you ultimately clean the bird. The fastest and easiest way is to simply filet the breast meat off the body, and remove the legs. This eliminates the need to eviscerate, skin or pluck the bird. Start by making an incision just under the skin, from the base of the breastbone up to the wishbone. Then, simply peel the skin back, exposing the breast meat. At the top of the breasts, you'll find a grayish-yellow gelatinous mass called a fat sponge. During the breeding season, gobblers spend more time breeding than feeding, and rely on this stored fat for energy. You can peel it away from the breast with your fingers, or cut it away with a knife. Next, filet the breasts off the breast bone, much as you would filet a fish.

Now you can peel the skin back around the drumsticks. Press the legs away from the body, popping the hip joint, then cut away any connecting tendons. If you haven't already done so, use a bone saw or knife to cut the second joint, separating the meaty portion of the drumstick from the scaly lower leg.

If you choose to keep the bird whole, for roasting or deep-fat frying, you will have to gut and pluck or skin the bird. To gut the bird, make an incision around the vent, being careful not to puncture any of the internal organs or guts. Then, simply reach inside the body cavity, grab hold of whatever's there, and pull it out. Next, use your fingernails to scrape out any remaining innards from between the ribs, along the back. Now, rinse out inside the body cavity. If you field-dress your bird in this manner, never rinse it in a stream, pond or lake, as this could introduce harmful bacteria.

Now for the outside. Skinning is the easier option, as you simply remove all the skin. However, unlike domestic birds, wild turkeys don't have much fat, and a skinned bird will dry out when cooking. It's important to baste repeatedly and often. You can also keep the breast moist by laying a few strips of bacon over it.

Plucking takes more work, but leaving the skin on helps retain what little fat there is in the skin. The sooner you pluck a bird, the easier it will be. Some folks will dip the bird in hot water before plucking, claiming that makes the job easier. I've never tried that so I really can't say. It is easier if you don't try to grab too many feathers at once, otherwise, you may rip the skin. Grab a few at a time and pull up and away, in the opposite direction the feathers lie. If you tie your own flies, or know someone who does, you may want to save some of the feathers for later use.

How you ultimately cook your bird is limited only by your own imagination. They taste great whether roasted, baked, smoked, deep-fat fried, chicken-fried...you name it. I don't claim to be any kind of gourmet chef—far from it. But necessity is the mother of invention, and having to deal with a half-dozen or more birds every spring has forced me to be inventive in creating, or finding, different recipes. Below are some of my favorites, including a few the folks at the National Wild Turkey Federation were kind enough to share with me.

CHICKEN-FRIED TURKEY

This is a simple and tasty way to prepare breast filets. I borrowed the concept from Brad Harris, of Outland Sports, but have customized it a bit for myself.

Ingredients:

1 (1-pound) boneless, skinless turkey breast, cut into 1-inch cubes

1 cup cornstarch

1 cup flour

2 eggs, beaten

spices to suit your taste

Directions:

In a shallow glass bowl, combine flour, cornstarch and spices. Beat eggs in another bowl. Oil and heat a large skillet. Dip turkey cubes into the eggs first, then into the flour and starch mixture. Throw them in the frying pan and cook until browned. Drain on a paper towel. Then serve. That's it!

TURKEY PATTIES

Ingredients:

1 (1-pound) ground boneless turkey meat (a good use for drumsticks and thighs)

2 eggs, beaten

1 cup seasoned bread crumbs

1 small chopped onion

1/2 teaspoons pepper

1/2 cup oatmeal

Directions: Combine all ingredients in a large bowl, mix thoroughly and form into patties. Place them on the grill and cook them just like you would hamburgers. Or, put them in a casserole dish, cover with cream of mushroom soup and bake at 350 degrees for one hour.

BAKED TURKEY BREAST

Here's a basic recipe for baked turkey breast that you can modify to the nth degree.

Ingredients:
1 (1-pound) skinless, boneless turkey breast
6 slices of bacon
1 teaspoons sweet basil
1 teaspoons paprika

Directions: Wash breast, pat dry, then place in an oiled casserole dish. Sprinkle on spices; then cover with bacon strips. Cover the dish and bake at 375 degrees for one hour, basting occasionally.

WILD TURKEY STIR-FRY

Stir-fry dishes are always a good choice when faced with feeding a family. Like the domestic chicken, turkey meat is a good choice for stir-fry dishes, and can add that extra flavor "kick" to a stir-fry recipe. Here is a great recipe from NWTF's *Wild About Turkey* cookbook.

Ingredients:
1/4 cup orange juice
$1^{1/2}$ tablespoons cornstarch
1 (1-pound) boneless, skinless turkey breast, cut into strips
3/4 cup chicken broth
$1^{1/2}$ tablespoons soy sauce
$2^{1/2}$ tablespoons vegetable oil
1 clove garlic, minced
$1^{1/2}$ teaspoons ground ginger
1 cup chopped broccoli
$1^{1/2}$ cup snow peas or green beans
1 medium red bell pepper, cut into thin strips
3/4 cup sliced green onion
1 medium carrot, cut into thin strips
2 cups cooked white or wild rice

Directions:

In a shallow glass bowl, combine orange juice and cornstarch. Add turkey, and stir to combine. Cover, and chill for 2 hours. Drain turkey, and discard juice mixture. Combine chicken broth and soy sauce. Set aside. In a wok or large skillet on medium heat, add oil, garlic and ginger. Stir-fry for 30 seconds. Add broccoli and next 4 ingredients, and stir-fry until crisp-tender, about 5 minutes. Stir in broth mixture. Simmer about 1 minute. Serve over rice. Yield: 4 servings

DEEP-FRIED WILD TURKEY

I've eaten wild turkey prepared in dozens of ways and nothing I've had yet beats a deep-fried bird. It takes a little more work, but is well worth the extra effort. Here are some tips for deep frying turkey from the National Wild Turkey Federation's *Wild About Turkey* cookbook:

- Always make sure the turkey is thawed completely.
- Clean the turkey in the same manner you would for roasting.
- Do not stuff the turkey when deep-frying.
- Either inject the turkey with liquid seasoning or rub dry sea sonings inside and out. Some examples include hot pepper sauce, black pepper, Italian dressing, Cajun seasonings and paprika.
- To determine how much oil to use in the deep fryer, fill the pot with water and lower the turkey into it. (Water should cover the turkey without spilling over.) Remove the turkey and measure the amount of water left in the pot. Discard the water and fill the pot with oil, after drying the pot thoroughly.
- Heat the oil to at least 310 degrees before adding the turkey.
- Skinless turkey should be cooked three minutes per pound, while turkey with skin should be cooked at 3 1/2 minutes per pound.
- Let the turkey cool for 20 to 30 minutes before carving.

CHEF ALBERT'S RED HOT TURKEY LEGS AND THIGHS

Ingredients:
Legs and thighs from one wild turkey
1 cup Redhot
1 cup BBQ sauce
1 cup chicken broth
2 tablespoons olive oil
1 teaspoon black pepper
Directions:

Separate legs from thighs into four pieces. Rub with olive oil and pepper. Brown on grill, place in aluminum foil pan, add sauces and broth. Cover and bring to boil on hot part of grill. Remove to indirect heat and cook for approximately 2 hours or until meat is tender and falls from the bone. Remove all bones and tendons, place meat back in sauce. Serve Pittsburgh style, on a toasted sesame bun with fries and coleslaw. Yields approximately one quart of pulled meat.

The *Wild About Turkey* cookbook has great wild turkey recipes and information, and can be purchased through NWTF's Turkey Shoppe, online at www.nwtf.org, or by calling 1-800-THE-NWTF.

Appendices

APPENDIX 1
Sources of Information

STATES:

Connecticut Department of
Environmental Protection
79 Elm Street
Hartford, CT 06106-5127
(860) 424-3555
www.dep.state.ct.us.

Maine Department of Inland
Fisheries & Wildlife
284 State Street
Augusta, ME 04333
(207) 287-2871
www.mefishwildlife.com

MassWildlife Field
Headquarters,Route 135
Westboro, MA 01582
(508) 792-7270
www.state.ma.us/dfwele/dfw.

Metropolitan District
Commission Division of
Watershed Management
Wachusett/Sudbury Section
PO Box 206
Clinton, MA 01510
(978) 365-2372
www.state.ma.us/mdc

New Hampshire Fish
& Game Department
2 Hazen Drive
Concord, NH 03301
(603) 271-3421
www.wildlife.state.nh.us

New Hampshire Division of
Parks & Recreation
PO Box 1856
172 Pembroke Road
Concord, NH 03302
(603) 271-3556
www.nhparks.state.nh.us

Rhode Island Department of
Environmental Management
Division of Fish & Wildlife
Great Swamp Field Headquarters
PO Box 281
West Kingston, RI 02892
(401) 789-0281

www.state.ri.us/dem/

Vermont Fish
& Wildlife Department
103 South Main Street
Waterbury, VT 05671-0501
(802) 241-3700.
www.anr.state.vt.us

Vermont Department of Forests,
Parks & Recreation
Montpelier, VT 05602
(802) 828-3375.
www.aec.state.vt

PRIVATE:
National Wild Turkey Federation
PO Box 530
Edgefield, SC 29824
(803) 637-3106
www.nwtf.org

MANUFACTURERS
Game Calls:
Hunter's Specialties
6000 Huntington Court NE
Cedar Rapids, IA 52402
(319) 395-0321
www.hunterspec.com

Knight & Hale Game Calls
PRADCO Outdoor Brands
3601 Jenny Lind Road
Fort Smith, AR 72901
(501) 782-8971
www.knight-hale.com

Lohman Game Calls, a division
of Outland Sports
4500 Doniphan Drive
Neosho, MO 64850
(417) 451-4438
www.outlandsports.com

MAD Calls, a division
of Outland Sports
4500 Doniphan Drive
Neosho, MO 64850
(417) 451-4438
www.outlandsports.com

Primos
604 First Street
Flora, MS 39071
(601) 879-9323
www.primos.com

Quaker Boy Game Calls
5455 Webster Road
Orchard Park, NY 14127
(800) 544-1600
www.quakerboygamecalls.com

Woods Wise Products
PO Box 681552
Franklin, TN 37068
(800) 735-8182
www.woodswise.com

Firearms/Ammunition:
Bennelli USA
17603 Indian Head Highway
Accokee, MD 20607
(301) 283-6981
www.benelliusa.com

Beretta USA
17601 Beretta Drive

Accokeek, MD 20607
(301) 283-2191
www.berettausa.com

Browning
One Browning Place
Morgan, UT 84050-9326
(801) 876-2711
www.browning.com

Connecticut Valley Arms
5988 Peachtree Comers E.
Norcross, GA 30071
(770) 449-4687
www.cva.com

Federal Cartridge Company
900 Ehlen Drive
Anoka, MN 55303
(763) 323-2300
www.federalcartridge.com

Knight Rifles
PO Box 130
Centerville, IA 52544
(641) 856-2626
www.knightrifles.com

O.F. Mossberg & Sons
7 Grasso Avenue
North Haven, CT 06473
(800) 989-GUNS
www.mossberg.com

Remington Arms
870 Remington Drive
Madison, NC 27025
(800) 243-9700
www.remington.com

Thompson/Center Arms
PO Box 5002
Rochester, NH 03866
(256) 463-5500
www.tcarms.com

Winchester
427 N. Shamrock Street
East Alton, IL 62024
(618) 258-3568
www.winchester.com

Decoys:

Feather Flex Decoys
4500 Doniphan Drive
Neosho, MO 64850
(417) 451-4438
www.outlandsports.com

Flambeau Product Corporation
PO Box 97
Middlefield, OH 44062
(800) 232-3474
www.flamprod.com

Outlaw Decoys
624 N. Fancher Road
Spokane, WA 99212
(800) OUTLAWS
www.outlaw.com

Catalogs:

Bass Pro Shops
2500 E. Kearney
Springfield, MO 65898
(800) BASS-PRO
www.basspro.com

Cabela's
One Cabela Drive
Sidney, NE 69160
(800) 237-4444
www.cabelas.com

Camouflage:
Bug-Out Outdoorwear
901 E. Stewart
Centerville, IA 52544
(877) 928-4688
www.bug-out-outdoorwear.com

Cover System
PortMidwest International
14570 Washington Road
West Burlington, Iowa 52655
(888) 419-6706
www.coversystem.com

Image Country Camouflage
14 Mountain Drive
Rutland, VT 05071
(800) 747-3009
www.imagecountry.com

Mossy Oak
Haas Outdoors, Inc.
PO Box 757
200 E. Main Street
West Point, MS 39773
(662) 494-8859
www.mossyoak.com

Natural Gear
5310 S. Shackleford, Suite D
Little Rock, AR 72204
(800) 590-5590
www.naturalgear.com

Predator, Inc.
2605 Coulee Ave.
Lacrosse WI 54601
(608) 787-0500
www.predatorcamo.com

Skyline Cover, LLC
S-3950 McKinley Parkway
Blasdell, NY 14219
(716) 649-2312
www.skylinecamo.com

Team Realtree
PO Box 9638
Columbus, GA 31908
(800) 992-9968
www.realtree.com

Timber Ghost
Ozark Mountain Outdoor Products
(800) 598-7106
www.timberghost.com

Trebark Camo Enterprises, Inc.
200 E. Main Street
West Point, MS 39773
(662) 494-8859
ww.trebark.com

Underbrush by Shelter-Pro
PO Box 337
Stearns, KY 42647
(606) 376-2004
www.underbrushblinds.com

Wacker Backer
Dept. PB
12261-D Cleveland

Nunica, MI 49448
(877) 922-5372
ww.wackerbacker.com.

Footwear:

Danner USA
18550 N.E. Riverside Parkway
Portland, OR 97230-4975
(800) 345-0430
www.danner.com

Elimitrax
3433 S. Campbell, Suite T
Springfield, MO 56807
(417) 888-6555

Georgia Boot
Irish Setter
314 Maine Street
Red Wing, MN 55066
(651) 385-1296
www.irishsetterboots.com

LaCrosse Footwear, Inc.
18550 NE Riverside Parkway
Portland, OR 97230
(800) 323-2668
www.lacrossefootwear.com

L.L Bean
Freeport, ME 04033
(800) 221-4221
www.llbean.com

The Muck Boot Company
1136 Second Street
Rock Island, IL 61201
(800) 777-9021
www.muckboot.com

Rocky Shoes and Boots
39 Canal Street
Nelsonville, OH 45764
(740) 753-1951
www.rockyboots.com

Wolverine
9341 Courtland Drive
Rockford, MI 49351
(616) 866-5500
www.wolverinebootsandshoes.com

Optics:

BSA Optics, Inc.
3911 S.W. 47th Avenue, Suite 914
Ft. Lauderdale, FL 33314
(954) 581-2144

Bushnell Sport Optics
9200 Cody
Overland Park, KS 66214-1734
(800) 423-3537
www.bushnell.com

Kahles
2 Slater Road
Cranston, RI 02920
(800) 606-8779
www.kahlesoptik.com

Tru-Glo, Inc.
PO Box 1612
McKinney, TX 75070
(922) 774-0300
www.trugloo.com

Mapping Software:

DeLorme Mapping Company
Two DeLorme Drive

Yarmouth, ME 04096
(800) 452-5931
www.delorme.com

MapTech
10 Industrial Way
Amesbury, MA 01913
(888) 839-5551
www.maptech.com

APPENDIX 2
TURKEY HUNTER'S CHECKLIST
Equipment

Vest
__ two box calls
__ two slates synthetic material
__ diaphragms
__ ziploc bag
__ strikers
__ shock call
__ decoys
__ stakes
__ screwdriver
__ turkey wing
__ call-care kit—chalk sandpaper and scrub pads
__ flashlight
__ compass
__ multi-purpose tool
__ knife
__ water bottle
__ bite-sized candy bars
__ toilet tissue in a ziploc bag

Clothing
__ extra face mask
__ camo gloves
__ boots
__ hat
__ pants
__ shirts
__ undershirts
__ poly pants
__ fleece sweatshirt
__ jacket
__ rubber boots
__ turkey boots
__ rain coat
__ rain pants
__ rain hat

Weaponry
__ shotgun
__ shells

Muzzleloader
__ gun
__ shot
__ powder
__ quickloads
__ wads
__ shot cups
__ primers
__ cleaning kit

Bow
__ bow
__ arrows
__ broadheads
__ stoppers
__ release

Other
__ blind
__ seat/stool
__ clippers/pruners
__ saw
__ stool
__ insect repellent
__ binoculars

glossary

ASSEMBLY CALL—The assembly call, or assembly yelp, is used by brood hens to gather their young in the event that the brood flock is separated. It is a highly variable call that may be soft or loud, and may contain a few single notes or a dozen or more.

BEARD—The beard is a hair-like appendage that protrudes from the central breast of predominantly male wild turkeys. The hair-like bristles are thought to be modified feathers. About four percent of hens have beards, and gobblers may occasionally lack them altogether. Turkeys typically sport one beard, but may have several.

BOSS GOBBLER—In spring flocks, the most dominant male, who dominates all others, is sometimes referred to as the Boss. During the breeding season, this bird will do most of the mating.

BOX CALL—A calling device consisting of a (typically) rectangular box and a hinged paddle. Sound is made by drawing the paddle across the side boards or rails of the box. Traditionally made of wood, box calls are now made of a variety of synthetic materials as well.

BROOD—The young, or poults, of a particular hen turkey.

CACKLE—The cackle is a rapid succession of loud, high-pitched staccato sounds that may vary in tone and rhythm. This call is often emitted by hens when they are flying into or out of the roost.

CALL-SHY—This term is sometimes applied to turkeys that have become conditioned to hunters' calling, and shy away when they hear it.

CLUCK—The cluck is a single-note call, which is more abrupt and less musical than a yelp. Similar in function to the yelp, the cluck attracts the attention of turkeys at a distance and helps keep the flock together.

CLUTCH–The hen turkey lays a clutch of eggs, typically ten to 12.

CUTT—When a turkey repeats a series of excited clucks it is referred to as "cutting." This call is most often used in the spring.

DIAPHRAGM—This is a mouth call consisting of three parts: a metal, horseshoe-shaped frame, a similarly-shaped tape skirt and a latex reed. It is held against the palate by pressing with the caller's tongue. Sound is made by gradually easing the pressure on the tongue, while simultaneously blowing a burst of air across the reed.

DRUMMING—This sound, sometimes referred to as the "spit-and-drum," begins with a sharp "spit" or "chuck" sound, followed by a deep, bassy sound a gobbler makes by resonating air in his chest. It is a short-range sound the gobbler makes while strutting.

DUSTING—Turkeys will often take dust baths to rid their body and feathers of ectoparasites like feather lice and mites. They often use traditional sites, and these will look like shallow, concave depressions in the bare earth.

FAN—The long retrices or tail feathers of the turkey can be spread out to form a fan, which gobblers do as part of their courtship display.

FIGHTING PURR—Alternately called the fighting "rattle," this is the sound made by male turkeys as they spar for dominance and breeding rights.

GOBBLE—This is the mating call of the male turkey, which he uses to attract hens. Toms and jakes may also gobble in response to a loud noise, a reaction called "shock–gobbling."

GOBBLER—A tom or jake, so called because of the gobbling call they make, most often during the mating season.

GOBBLER YELP—Gobblers also yelp, though less often than hens. Their yelps are usually deeper in tone, coarser, and often more spaced out than those of hens. They can sometimes be used to attract bachelor groups of male birds in the fall.

HENNED-UP—Once a tom has gathered his harem of hens, it can be very difficult to call him away. Such a bird is described as being "henned-up."

HUNG-UP—Toms will often gobble to a hunter's calls, and move in his direction, only to stop or "hang up" out of range.

JAKE—A jake is a juvenile male turkey. This term is generally applied to young males after they have entered their first spring, and sport beards of four to six inches.

JENNY—A jenny is a juvenile female turkey.

KEE-KEE—This call consists of a series of very high-pitched, whistle-like notes that turkeys emit in a rhythmic fashion—the number of notes or syllables ranging from a few to over ten. It is an assembly call, emitted by a young turkey when it has become lost or separated from a flock or family group.

KEE-KEE RUN—This call consists of a series of kee-kee calls followed immediately by several yelps, and simulates a young turkey that is learning how to yelp.

LOST CALL—The lost call or yelp is a long call having as many as 30 notes or syllables. Louder and lower-pitched than the plain yelp, it is characterized by urgent tonal inflections. This call is used in the fall to regroup a scattered flock.

LIMBHANGER—As a turkey's spurs grow longer, they become sharper and more hooked. Older turkeys, whose spurs are long and hooked enough to allow the bird to be hung from a tree limb, are called limbhangers.

MOLT—Molting is the process by which feathers are systematically lost and replaced.

PATTERNING—This is the process of test–firing a shotgun to determine its accuracy, and the relative shot density (pattern) of particular loads.

PECKING ORDER—The social organization of local turkey flocks is governed by a linear, dominance hierarchy or "pecking order," wherein each bird dominates those of lesser social rank.

PLAIN YELP—This is emitted by turkeys while in the trees or on the ground. It is longer (sometimes more than ten syllables or notes) and much louder than the tree yelp. It is believed that birds use this call later in the day in order to keep the flock together. When effectively imitated by hunters in the fall, the plain yelp can sometimes be used to attract gobblers or hens.

POULT—Young turkeys, less than four months of age are referred to as poults.

PRIMARY FEATHERS—Primary feathers are the long flight feathers of the wings.

PURR—The purr is usually described as a one-second-long, soft, medium-pitched sound. This low level purring is often emitted by members of a contented, undisturbed flock, particularly when they are feeding.

PUSH-PIN CALL—Alternately called the push-button call, it consists of a wooden box with a striker mounted inside. A wooden, spring-loaded dowel, with a small paddle attached, is then mounted through two holes in either end of the box. The call is operated by pushing the peg with one finger, which draws the paddle across the striker.

PUTT—If the flock is disturbed, the cluck may change to a louder putt call or to a very loud putting, which expresses aggression or fear. Using this call will usually alarm turkeys rather than attracting them.

ROOST—From the time they are old enough to fly, turkeys will roost in trees at night for security. They often use the same tree or trees, which are referred to as a roost.

SCRATCHINGS—Turkeys often feed by scratching away leaves and duff to uncover seeds, nuts and insects. In doing so, they leave "v–shaped" patches of bare ground.

SHOCK CALL—Hunters can sometimes coax a turkey into gobbling by blowing a loud a crow, peacock, coyote or pileated woodpecker call. The response is termed a "shock gobble."

SLATE—This calling device typically consists of a slate disc, mounted in a wooden bowl, or pot, though there are numerous variations in shapes and materials. Calls are made by drawing a wooden (or synthetic) peg across the surface.

SNOOD—The front of a gobbler's head is also adorned with a slender, fleshy appendage at the base of the bill. Called a snood, it becomes elongated and dangles beside the head when the bird is excited.

SNUFF BOX—A type of tube call that is made by stretching a sheet of latex over the open top of a snuff can.

SPURS—Males sport spurs, sharp, curved appendages on the rear of their metatarsus (lower leg). Those of a jake will typically be short and rounded. Females generally lack them.

STRUTTING—This is the mating display of the male wild turkey. He begins by erecting, or puffing up, his body feathers. He simultaneously lifts his tail perpendicular to the ground and spreads out his tail feathers to form a full fan, as he spreads and lowers his wings so the outer primaries drag on the ground. In this pose, he will take two or three quick steps, then utter a sharp "spit" sound followed by a low-pitched hum.

STRUT ZONE—A tom will often pick a specific location, like a logging road, topographical bench or a field, where he will pace back and forth, performing his courtship display.

TOM—This term is typically applied to an adult male turkey that is two years old or older.

TREE YELP—Early in the morning, while still on the roost, wild turkeys sometimes emit a soft, three to four note yelp. This call functions as a form of communication between birds while on the roost. Hunters might use this call as a signal to turkeys that there are other birds roosted nearby.

TROLLING—This is the technique of traveling along, stopping every 100 to 200 yards to call, in hopes of eliciting a gobble.

TUBE—Similar to the snuff-box, this call consists of a latex reed stretched over the opening of a tube.

WINGBONE CALL—This is a mouth call, operated by sucking air through a narrow tube made of turkey wing bones.

YELP—The most common and basic turkey call is a "yelp." Yelps consist of a series of two-note "kee-yuk"calls that hens emit in a rhythmic fashion, typically repeated five to seven times, but often much more. The three most common types of yelps are the: tree yelp, plain yelp and lost call or assembly call.

the end

- **Baño entero de agua enfriada:** Este baño de efecto tónico, primero se prepara con agua caliente o tibia y después se añade poco a poco agua fría, sin que alcance una temperatura inferior a los 20° C.

- **Baño entero de agua caliente:** Este baño tiene un efecto sedante y facilita la conciliación del sueño estando el agua entre los 35° C y los 38° C. También puede ser realizado con una temperatura superior a los 38° C, es decir, por encima de la temperatura corporal (provocando una aceleración del pulso y de la respiración que se ve acompañada por una gran sudoración).

- **Baños parciales:** Los baños parciales se centran en una sola parte del cuerpo. Los baños parciales de agua fría resultan óptimos para combatir los estados congestivos del hígado y el bazo, así como los trastornos gastrointestinales, entre otros, siendo contraindicado para aquellas personas que padecen enfermedades renales. Los baños parciales de agua caliente son indicados para las personas que padecen cólicos viscerales o dolores rectales, entre otros.

- **Duchas frías:** Las duchas de agua fría (de 10° C a 14° C de temperatura) templan el organismo y ayudan a evitar la bronquitis o los catarros, además de activar el recambio orgánico.

- **Duchas calientes:** Estas duchas de agua caliente (entre los 30° C y los 35° C) poseen una acción benéfica y relajante sobre todo el organismo, siendo, además, sedantes del sistema nervioso vegetativo.

- **Baños turcos o saunas de vapor de agua:** Las saunas permiten aumentar la sudoración y, por ello, incrementan la eliminación de las toxinas. Suelen ir acompañadas de duchas de agua fría.

La hidroterapia es un método que no es difícil ni costoso, ya que simplemente en nuestro propio hogar podemos realizar muchos de los ejercicios. A continuación le mostramos algunos de los posibles procedimientos que puede realizar para obtener una relajación a través de la hidroterapia.

Preparación de un baño entero relajante. Si se encuentra fatigado o tenso, ya sea física o mentalmente, puede prepararse un baño relajante para eliminar toda tensión acumulada. Además de descansar la mente, los músculos se distensionarán y relajarán. Le recomendamos que tras el baño, se relaje unos minutos sobre la cama o en un lugar donde se encuentre especialmente cómodo, pues así los efectos relajantes se verán potenciados.

Dúchese primero, con agua más fría que caliente, para que la piel se limpie y los poros se abran. A continuación, prepare una bañera con agua caliente, sin exceder los 37° C (pues es la temperatura interna del cuerpo humano), y añada aceite esencial de alguna planta que favorezca la relajación, como lavanda, manzanilla, sándalo o rosa (para más información *véase* el apartado de aromaterapia, páginas 125 a 127). Sumerja todo el cuerpo en el agua, excepto la cabeza, y lleve a cabo algún ejercicio de respiración mientras masajea el plexo solar, entre el abdomen y el pecho, con movimientos circulares lentos, en sentido contrario a las agujas del reloj. Siempre que le sea posible, permanezca diez minutos dentro del agua. Uno o dos baños completos semanales serán óptimos para aquellas personas con trastornos de sueño, pues el agua templada (entre 33° C y 38° C) relajará los músculos y le permitirá dormir mejor.

Preparación de baños parciales relajantes. Si no dispone de tiempo para un baño entero, puede realizar baños parciales de distintas partes del cuerpo.

Uno de los más empleados y aconsejados es el baño parcial de pies. Según la reflexología, en la planta de los pies se refleja todo el organismo, desde la columna vertebral a los ojos. Bastará sentarse, de forma que ninguna parte del cuerpo esté tensa, y sumergir los pies en agua caliente (entre 36º C y 37º C de temperatura), a la que puede añadir algún aceite o un buen puñado de sal marina.

Si padece trastornos de sueño, sumerja las piernas hasta las rodillas antes de acostarse. El agua fría conducirá la sangre hasta los muslos y aumentará el riego sanguíneo de las piernas. Sin embargo, si siempre tiene los pies fríos, deberá alternar los baños parciales de piernas en agua caliente, durante tres o cinco minutos, y en agua fría, sólo un minuto.

Relajarse estimulando los nervios. Las investigaciones han demostrado que los nervios necesitan tensarse para después distensionarse. Todos los nervios del cuerpo están interrelacionados. Mientras unos se encargan de captar los estímulos del exterior, otros transmiten las señales que reciben. Es importante estimularlos, pues –a diferencia de todas las demás células del cuerpo humano– las células nerviosas no se renuevan, siendo las mismas a lo largo de nuestra vida. Someter los nervios a cambios de temperatura o de humedad provoca un aumento de la actividad emisora.

A continuación le mostramos una serie de procedimientos para estimular la tensión de los nervios y, como consecuencia, para obtener una relajación corporal completa.

- Al levantarse, lávese todo el cuerpo con una toallita humedecida en agua fría, primero las extremidades (primero las piernas y luego los brazos, incluyendo tanto las plantas de los pies como los dedos de las manos) y después el tronco y la nuca. Si lo prefiere, realice este procedimiento bajo una ducha de agua templada, seguida, en lo posible, por una ducha localizada de agua fría.

- Después de la jornada laboral, sumérjase en una bañera con agua fría (cuidando que los pies estén bien calientes), de forma que le cubra hasta la pantorrilla, y chapotee. Si lo prefiere, realice un baño de pies (de forma que el agua llegue a las rodillas), primero en agua caliente durante unos minutos y después en agua fría, sólo durante unos segundos.
- Dos veces por semana y antes de acostarse, haga un baño parcial con agua fría de brazos, sumergidos hasta los codos.

Musicoterapia

Es una técnica que emplea la música para fomentar el bienestar y la relajación, siendo también una valiosa herramienta para el desarrollo personal. Esta práctica suele estar muy ligada a la aromaterapia, pues incrementa la percepción de los beneficios de los aceites. Asimismo, también es empleada como un método auxiliar para terapias médicas o relajantes, dado que crea un ambiente relajante que facilita el tratamiento.

A través de la música se pueden estimular diferentes áreas del cerebro, permitiendo un mejor dominio corporal y un restablecimiento de los ritmos fisiológicos del propio organismo. La musicoterapia estudia la tonalidad, la armonía, la melodía y la resonancia.

Los egipcios, en la Antigüedad, creían que la música incrementaba la fertilidad de las mujeres. En la actualidad, algunas investigaciones han demostrado que aquellos bebes que escucharon música clásica en el vientre de su madre nacieron muchos más tranquilos.

Le recomendamos que escuche sonidos que le resulten agradables. Podrá comprobar que esto le ayudará a alcanzar una mayor relajación.

Adopte una postura que le resulte cómoda y escuche alguna obra específica para la relajación. Después, póngase de pie cerca de los altavoces y acompase la respiración con la música, con lo que aumentará su sensibilidad corporal. A continuación túmbese de nuevo y relájese.

De forma similar, cuando se encuentre incómodo o bajo de ánimo, escuchar música alegre le aportará vitalidad.

Obras relajantes. Éstas son algunas de las obras relajantes que se emplean en musicoterapia:

- Clásica
  - Claudio Monteverdi: Orfeo ed Euridice (en especial la introducción y el primer acto).
  - John Dowland: Integral de obras para laúd.
  - Luys Díaz: Los seis libros del delfín de música.
  - L. van Beethoven: Adagio del concierto número 5, El emperador; sinfonía número 6, «Pastoral».
  - G.F. Haendel: largo de la ópera Kercós; Música para los reales fuegos de artificio.
  - Schubert: Rosamunda.

- Ambiental y «New Age»
  - Philip Chapman: Return of Angels.
  - Mike Rowland: The Fairy Ring; Titania; Silver Wings.
  - Deuter: Sands of Time; Cicada.
  - Patrick Ball: Secret Isles, O'Carolan's Dream.
  - Kitaro: Silk Road; Best of Kitaro.
  - Daniel Kobialka: Going Home; Oh What A Beautiful Morning.
  - Steven Halpern: Spectrum Suite; Higher Ground.
  - Aeoliah: Love in the Wind; Inner Sanctum.
  - Paul Horn: Inside the Taj Mahal; Nomad.
  - Tony Scott: Music for Zen meditation.
  - Raphael: Music to disappear in.

Meditación y visualización

Meditación

¿Qué es la meditación? La meditación es una técnica que vacía la mente de todo pensamiento, permitiéndonos olvidar todas las preocupaciones, ya sean del trabajo, familiares, del entorno o respecto nosotros mismos. Se diferencia de la relajación por tratarse de un proceso activo. A pesar de que es necesaria la relajación para practicar la meditación y aunque con la meditación también se obtiene una relajación física y mental, la meditación es un proceso activo, pues la persona que la practica dirige de forma consciente su atención al objeto de meditación.

Gracias a la meditación, se consigue descargar las tensiones y por tanto, obtener una relajación física, al mismo tiempo que se desarrolla de forma gradual la habilidad de observar y controlar los propios pensamientos. Además, mediante esta técnica podemos trascender el nivel de conciencia que empleamos normalmente durante el día y conocer los pensamientos inconscientes.

No olvidemos que si aprendemos a equilibrar la mente y el cuerpo, podremos reconocer los desequilibrios internos cuando aparezcan y así restablecernos en el presente y prevenir los posibles contratiempos en el futuro.

Durante siglos, las religiones de todo el mundo han usado la meditación para comunicarse con las diferentes divinidades. Basada en los principios de la medicina terapéutica oriental, la meditación está presente tanto en el hinduismo, como en el budismo, el sufismo, el zen o el cristianismo.

Asimismo, la meditación es la base de todas las clases de Yoga. Mientras que el Yoga parte de una relajación física para obtener una relajación mental, la meditación parte de la relajación mental para obtener la relajación física. Ambas técnicas están estrechamente unidas, pues durante la práctica del Yoga la mente debe permanecer en calma, obteniéndose mayores beneficios si se encuentra centrada en un solo pensamiento. A través de la meditación, el yogui cultiva la atención pura, aprende a controlar sus reacciones, alcanza una visión clara, unifica la conciencia, purifica el subconsciente y combate todos los pensamientos o reacciones mecánicas.

La meditación en las filosofías orientales. La visión del cuerpo humano en el pensamiento oriental ayuda a comprender la esencia de la meditación.

Según los yoguis, el hinduísmo o el Tantra, por ejemplo, el ser humano es una condensación de energías que fluyen tanto a través de los canales por los que circula la energía vital del cuerpo (denominados *nadis*), como a través de unos puntos de concentración energética (los *chakras*). Mediante la meditación –unida a ciertas técnicas específicas– el discípulo puede conservar la energía o fuerza vital, purificar los nadis y reactivar los chakras, alcanzando un equilibrio entre el cuerpo y la mente.

La meditación es tanto la supresión de los pensamientos, como el pensamiento correcto. Así pues, la meditación constituye una de las disciplinas con las que se puede, por una parte, abrir la mente a otras realidades y, por otra parte, alcanzar un nuevo estado de la consciencia.

Un gran número de investigaciones científicas han demostrado los profundos efectos positivos de la meditación y del Yoga, tanto para la presión sanguínea, como para la tensión muscular y el corazón, así como para combatir la ansiedad, la fatiga o la depresión.

Durante la meditación el cuerpo se vuelve más pesado y la respiración se hace más lenta y profunda. Además, paulatinamente la mente se aleja tanto del cuerpo como del entorno. Llevar a cabo una sesión de veinte minutos de meditación, una o dos veces cada día, permite reducir el consumo de oxígeno y la producción de anhídrido carbónico en un 20%, disminuye la presión sanguínea y el nivel de lactosa en la sangre.

La actividad cerebral y la meditación. Las investigaciones han demostrado que la meditación permite que el cerebro consiga un equilibrio entre las ondas alfa y theta. Es decir, el cuerpo adquiere un estado de relajación profunda, mientras que la mente, a pesar de seguir despierta y alerta, también alcanza un estado de relajación plena.

Durante la meditación, el individuo se libera tanto de los bloqueos físicos como de las tensiones emocionales. El cuerpo adopta entonces la llamada «reacción de relajación», opuesta a la «reacción de lucha o huida» provocada por el estrés (*véase* el apartado del estrés, página 9).

¿Qué fin tienen las técnicas de meditación? La finalidad de las técnicas de meditación dependerá de la persona que las realice y del momento de su vida en el que se encuentre. Quizás en un principio las utilice para curar una dolencia específica relacionada con el estrés y, después, para algún fin más espiritual.

Aunque innumerables, las metas de la meditación pueden ser divididas en prácticas, médicas o espirituales. En primer lugar, la meditación tiene una finalidad práctica cuando sirve de ayuda para realizar una acción. Así, es la base de muchas técnicas tradicionales de artes marciales, siendo también empleada por los deportistas para aumentar la concentración y el rendimiento (tanto por atletas profesionales como por aquellas personas que practican usualmente algún deporte), por los músicos, los actores y los bailarines para desarrollar la creatividad y para preparar su actuación sobre el escenario. De la misma forma, muchos estudiantes también emplean técnicas de meditación para eliminar la tensión, aumentar su capacidad de concentración y preparar los exámenes.

Por otra parte, la meditación también se emplea con finalidades médicas, incluyendo todo tipo de terapias y curaciones específicas, así como para conservar la salud y el bienestar. Gracias a esta técnica es posible aliviar dolores localizados, curar enfermedades psicosomáticas y ayudar en aquellos casos en los que las enfermedades se ven agravadas por desórdenes emocionales.

Por último, a través de la meditación se puede crear un equilibrio entre el cuerpo, la mente y las emociones.

Las técnicas de meditación. La meditación puede no basarse en objetos y realizarse sin necesidad de complicadas posturas físicas, sino sólo sentándose. Sin embargo, la meditación no implica necesariamente sentarse con las piernas cruzadas y repetir constantemente ciertas palabras, aunque algunas personas la alcancen así.

En realidad, existe un gran número de técnicas para conseguir la meditación, entre las que podríamos destacar las siguientes: la concentración de la mente en un objeto, un sonido, una figura geométrica, un color o un concepto; la percepción y concentración en el silencio interno; ejercicios de visualización para propiciar un estado anímico positivo; así como técnicas de percepción de una acción del propio cuerpo o de la mente, sin interpretar lo percibido. Así pues, el centro de la meditación será diferente para cada persona, pudiendo ser, por ejemplo, una flor, una vela, un sonido o la propia respiración. Por otra parte, la meditación puede realizarse adquiriendo una determinada postura, aunque también a través del movimiento de la danza.

Desde hace miles de años, también se han empleado en las religiones orientales otras técnicas de meditación como los mantras, los mandalas o el koan.

Los mantras son sonidos de una o más sílabas, que se considera que representan a ciertos pensamientos sagrados o plegarias y que deben repetirse con plena comprensión de su significado. El mantra permite la concentración rigurosa de la mente tanto en el propio mantra, como en aquello que éste simboliza. No son oraciones para adorar o suplicar algo a la divinidad, sino formas pronunciadas según rigurosas normas de ritmo y acentuación, cuya finalidad es conectar el ser individual con el ser supremo. Estos sonidos específicos producen resonancias que, a su vez, combinadas con el ritmo del mantra, amplían la conciencia y elevan el entendimiento.

Según el budismo y el hinduismo, los mantras espirituales hacen presente en el ser individual a la deidad específica, cuya esencia sonora es similar al mantra emitido. Existe un enorme número de mantras, siendo diferente la función de cada uno. Así, hay mantras de curación, de poder, místicos o aquellos que invocan al ser interior o a la energía cósmica.

Por otra parte, los mandalas son la representación visual de los mantras. Son figuras geométricas que representan ciertas imágenes simbólicas y cuya finalidad es ayudar a la concentración y a la contemplación. No existen dos mandalas iguales, pues muestran la situación psíquica de su autor y la aportación que éste realiza a la idea tradicional. Los componentes básicos de todos son inalterables, encontrándose siempre el punto, la línea, el círculo, el cuadrado, el triángulo y el símbolo del loto.

Finalmente, los koan son preguntas que no pueden ser respondidas mediante la razón y la lógica. Son empleados para la meditación, sobre todo en el budismo zen, pues amplían el pensamiento, estimulan la intuición y promueven la meditación. Uno de los koans más antiguos y conocidos, todavía empleado en las sesiones de meditación, es el siguiente: «*¿Qué sonido tiene una palmada dada con una sola mano?*».

POSICIONES Y PASOS PREVIOS A LAS TÉCNICAS DE MEDITACIÓN

Para meditar de forma correcta, es necesario encontrarse en un lugar tranquilo, adoptar una postura relajada y tener una actitud meditativa.

Así, debe situarse en un lugar en el que exista tranquilidad y donde pueda estar solo durante media hora por lo menos. Por ello debe seguir las mismas pautas explicadas al principio del capítulo anterior.

El objetivo de la meditación es obtener un equilibrio entre la mente y el cuerpo, por lo que es muy importante adoptar una posición correcta. No existe una sola postura correcta, sino que ésta dependerá de cada uno. Ya sea sentado o estirado, el cuerpo debe estar relajado, sin crearle molestias, calambres o entumecimiento. Por ello, si padece tensión en la espalda o en las extremidades, puede tenderse en el suelo. Sin embargo, tampoco debe estar cómodo en exceso, pues podría quedarse dormido. A algunas personas les gusta sentarse en una silla, mientras que otras prefieren sentarse en el suelo o adoptar la posición del loto.

A continuación le mostramos la forma correcta de adoptar diferentes posturas para obtener una meditación plena.

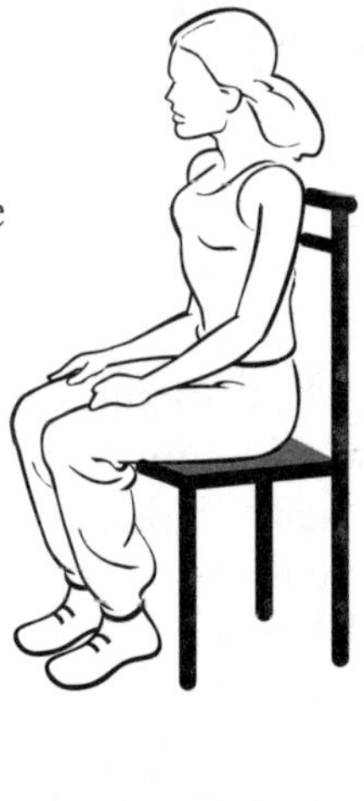

Sentarse en una silla

Para adoptar esta postura, elija una silla de respaldo duro, en la que pueda apoyar la espalda hasta la mitad. Una vez sentado en ella, las piernas no deben colgar sueltas, sino que las plantas de los pies deben tocar el suelo. Deje descansar las manos suavemente en su regazo y relaje las piernas, ya sea manteniéndolas unidas o separadas. La espalda debe permanecer recta y la cabeza erguida.

Sentarse en el suelo

Siéntese en el suelo, con la espalda recta y la cabeza erguida. Descanse las manos sobre los muslos, de forma que las note relajadas. Por su parte, las piernas deben permanecer extendidas hacia delante. Junte las rodillas y los pies. Para que la espalda no pueda encorvarse, apóyela en la pared.

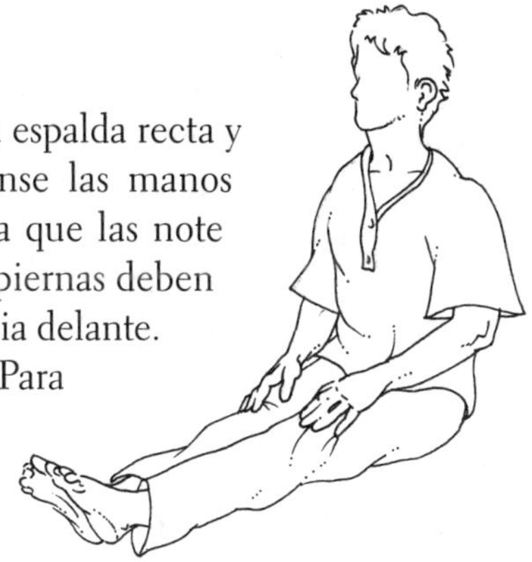

Posición de piernas cruzadas

Siéntese en el suelo, con la espalda recta, la cabeza erguida y las piernas extendidas hacia delante. Con las manos presionando ligeramente el suelo, cruce ambas piernas hasta conseguir una postura que le resulte cómoda. Enderece la columna y presione ligeramente hacia delante. Luego descanse las manos sobre las rodillas, con las palmas hacia abajo o hacia arriba, según prefiera.

Posición del loto

En el Yoga, ésta es una de las posturas básicas para sentarse. Recibe este nombre porque la posición de las manos y de los pies recuerda los pétalos del loto. Para realizarla, siéntese con las piernas hacia delante y extiéndalas. Después, doble la pierna izquierda llevando el talón a la ingle y levante el pie hasta la parte superior del muslo derecho. Haga lo mismo con la pierna derecha, de forma que el pie derecho descanse sobre el muslo izquierdo. Enderece la columna y presione ligeramente hacia delante. La posición se mantendrá sola. Por último, cierre los ojos. Esta postura resulta óptima para la meditación, corrigiendo también las posturas erróneas que pueda adoptar.

Posición del medio loto

Si le resulta difícil adoptar la postura anterior, puede realizar la posición del medio loto. Para ello, siéntese con las piernas extendidas. A continuación, doble la pierna derecha, colocando el pie junto a la ingle izquierda y levante el pie hasta la parte superior del muslo derecho. Después, doble la pierna izquierda, situando el pie debajo de la pierna derecha. Enderece la columna vertebral y mantenga la cabeza y el cuello erguidos. Por último, cierre los ojos.

Estirarse

Estírese en el suelo o en una cama, de forma que la columna vertebral esté recta. Las manos deben reposar a ambos lados del cuerpo, mientras que los hombros y el cuello deben estar completamente relajados.

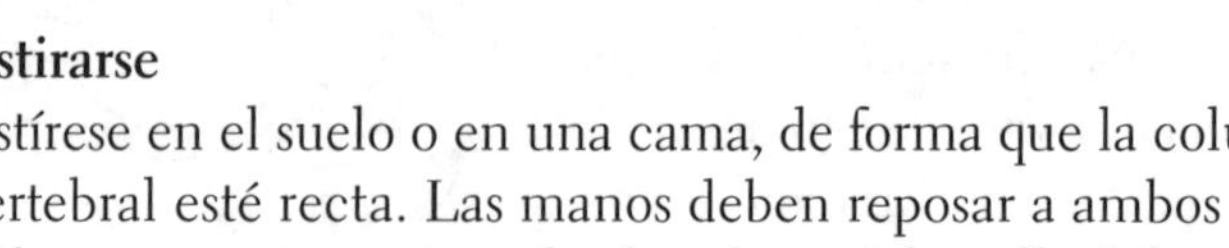

Una vez elegida la postura que le resulte más cómoda, debe realizar los siguientes pasos para comenzar los ejercicios de meditación:

- La respiración no debe ser forzada, sino lenta y profunda.
- Lleve a cabo cinco respiraciones completas, mientras repasa todos los pensamientos que le preocupan en ese momento, sin forzar ninguna idea ni intentar suprimirla.
- Poco a poco irá consiguiendo que los pensamientos desaparezcan de su mente, expulsándolos con cada espiración.
- Concentre el pensamiento en el ritmo de su respiración o en algún objeto, intentando ser perseverante. Ésta no es una práctica estricta que conlleve mucho esfuerzo, sino que debe permitir que todos los pensamientos sean absorbidos por el objeto de meditación.
- Cuando haya conseguido que su mente esté en blanco o haya suprimido todos los pensamientos, intente alargar todo lo posible ese espacio de tiempo, procurando siempre que su mente esté vacía y en silencio. Cuando tenga más práctica, podrá repetir este ejercicio para sosegar la mente siempre que lo necesite.
- Una vez alcanzado este estado de meditación en silencio, debe respirar profundamente, poco a poco, para dejar este estado y reanudar la actividad normal de una forma correcta. Después de tres respiraciones lentas, mueva lentamente los pies, las manos, los brazos y las piernas. Sólo entonces abrirá los ojos y se levantará muy lentamente hasta ponerse de pie.

TÉCNICAS DE MEDITACIÓN PARA GENTE MUY OCUPADA

Ante todo, debe elegir una postura en la que pueda sentirse cómodo durante toda la meditación, sin que pueda empezar a sentir dolor en las rodillas o en la espalda tras cinco minutos. Es importante que la mente no se entretenga en los problemas del trabajo o familiares, pues no se relajaría. Después, elija una concentración que no le agote o un mantra sencillo. Lea los ejercicios siguientes y elija el que le parezca más adecuado para usted. Le aconsejamos que pruebe distintas técnicas, pues así descubrirá cuál de ellas tiene unos efectos más convenientes para usted en ese momento.

Dejar la mente en blanco

Al principio, puede sentirse muy desanimado al verse incapaz de llevar la mente a un estado de vacío. Por ello, el primer paso para iniciarse en la práctica de la meditación es limpiar el subconsciente y liberar así la mente de los muchos pensamientos que puedan surgir.

El siguiente ejercicio consiste en seguir los tres niveles del proceso del control de los pensamientos y expansión de la mente, basados en la meditación yóguica.

Primero debe realizar un proceso de observación de los pensamientos (basado en el primer nivel denominado *pratyarhar*), intentando verlos desde fuera, es decir, sin tomar partido. Esto le conducirá a descartar todo pensamiento que pueda impedir la meditación.

Seguidamente, debe fijar la mente en un solo punto, de forma que le sea posible detener o fijar la dirección de sus pensamientos. Esta práctica (llamada *dharana*), le permitirá fijar la mente hasta conseguir detener «el diálogo interno». Con este fin, puede utilizar una concentración visual en un objeto que sea de su agrado, una concentración en ciertas palabras o mantras, o una concentración sensorial que dirija la atención a ciertas partes del cuerpo o al proceso respiratorio.

Por último, con la meditación propiamente dicha (denominada dhyana) podrá orientar y controlar sus pensamientos, obteniendo así una relajación tanto física como mental y emocional.

Meditar con la mente concentrada en un objeto

1. Siéntese adoptando algunas de las posturas arriba mencionadas.

2. Coloque una flor, una vela o cualquier objeto que sea de su agrado a cierta distancia de usted. Concentre toda su atención en dicho objeto mientras toma conciencia de su propia respiración. Recuerde que no debe forzar la respiración, sino observar como sube y baja la caja torácica, sin intentar controlarla.
3. Concéntrese en el objeto. Si le vienen a la mente ciertos pensamientos, no intente luchar contra ellos, sino que permita que fluyan sin dejar nunca de concentrarse en el objeto.
4. Cuando haya conseguido mantener fija su atención durante cierto tiempo sin verse interrumpido, cierre los ojos. A continuación, centre su atención en la imagen de dicho objeto. Observe los detalles del mismo, hasta que la imagen desaparezca. Si al cerrar los ojos no ve con claridad el objeto de su meditación, vuelva a abrir los ojos y repita el proceso.
5. Con los ojos ya abiertos, realice unas respiraciones profundas y lentas antes de empezar a mover su cuerpo lentamente para abandonar la meditación.

Meditar con la mente centrada en la propia respiración

- Siga los mismos pasos que en el ejercicio anterior, pero con la mente centrada en su propia respiración. Para ello, observe cómo inspira por la nariz, sintiendo cómo entra el aire en el abdomen, hasta llenar por completo los pulmones.
- Permanezca unos segundos antes de expulsar el aire con suavidad. Luego tense los músculos del abdomen y permanezca así unos segundos. Repita este proceso, intentando imaginarse cómo la energía recorre su cuerpo al inspirar y lo abandona al espirar.

Meditar con la mente centrada en un mantra

- Para meditar puede centrar su atención en un objeto o en la propia respiración, pero también en una determinada palabra o mantra. Esta palabra actuará como punto de referencia para no distraerse en otros pensamientos o preocupaciones. Debe elegir una palabra que le transmita un estado de ánimo positivo, ya sea de su propia cosecha o utilizando algún mantra tradicional. En el Yoga, la sílaba sánscrita «*om*» es considerada como el mantra superior. La pronunciación de esta sílaba, apoyándose en una respiración adecuada, permite liberar la mente e inundar la conciencia.

- Siéntese adoptando algunas de las posturas arriba mencionadas y cierre los ojos. Concentre toda su atención en la palabra que haya escogido, mientras toma conciencia de su propia respiración. Recuerde que no debe forzar la respiración, sino observar cómo sube y baja la caja torácica, sin intentar controlarla.
- Pronuncie la palabra cada vez que expulse el aire, alargando el sonido hasta que sus pulmones se hayan vaciado por completo.
- Si le vienen a la mente ciertas ideas, no intente luchar contra ellas, permita que fluyan sin dejar nunca de concentrarse en el mantra. Cuando haya conseguido mantener fija su atención durante algún tiempo sin verse interrumpido, permanezca así todo el tiempo que le sea posible.
- Después, deje que la palabra se desvanezca de su mente, realice unas respiraciones profundas y abra los ojos.
- Por último, mueva su cuerpo lentamente para abandonar la meditación.

Visualización

Es una técnica de relajación mediante la cual se traen a la mente ciertas imágenes relajantes, como puede ser la infinitud del mar en un día soleado, un bosque en primavera, etcétera.

Unida a determinadas técnicas, la visualización permite contrarrestar el nerviosismo, la ansiedad, los miedos o un estado de ánimo pesimista. Mediante imágenes positivas, podemos reemplazar los pensamientos negativos y enfrentarnos con mayor confianza en nosotros mismos a las situaciones difíciles, al dolor, etcétera. De hecho, algunas técnicas de visualización permiten conseguir un equilibrio entre el hemisferio izquierdo del cerebro y el derecho, agudizando tanto la memoria como los sentidos.

- Para llevar a cabo las visualizaciones debe adoptar las mismas posturas que para la meditación, concentrándose en poner la mente en blanco, seguir un sonido o el ritmo de la propia respiración.

- Las imágenes a evocar dependerán de cada persona. Así, puede imaginarse un riachuelo en la montaña, o, si padece alguna enfermedad o dolor, puede imaginar cómo se sentiría si estas afecciones no existieran. Es decir, podemos conducir la mente para relajar aquellos aspectos mentales o emocionales que se encuentran tensos.

- Después de realizar varias respiraciones profundas, debe concentrarse en la imagen que ha elegido, volviendo a ella cada vez que se dé cuenta que la mente se centra en otros pensamientos. Al principio se sorprenderá de lo indisciplinados que son los pensamientos, pero con la práctica, será capaz de permanecer concentrado en un solo pensamiento tanto tiempo como desee. Por ello, al principio, los ejercicios deben ser de cinco o diez minutos, incrementándose de forma gradual hasta alcanzar una media hora.

- Si practica la visualización con regularidad, mejorará su capacidad de concentración y aprendizaje combatiendo de forma más fácil toda tensión o estrés.

EJERCICIOS DE VISUALIZACIÓN

Crear una visualización para liberarse del estrés

A principios de los años setenta, esta técnica empezó a ser utilizada por los terapeutas de la llamada Programación Neurolingüística (PNL), disciplina que estudiaba tantos los procesos neurológicos de todos los sentidos, como los procesos de comunicación verbal y no verbal y las elecciones de comportamientos. A través de esta técnica podrá desencadenar un efecto psicológico que reactive una sensación de relajación. Por ello, podrá utilizarla siempre que se encuentre tenso. Muchas personas consideran esta técnica especialmente eficaz, pues cada persona elige su propia fantasía para relajarse.

- Adopte alguna postura cómoda en la que se encuentre relajado. Le aconsejamos que elija alguna de las posturas mencionadas en el apartado de la meditación.
- A continuación, cierre los ojos e intente pensar en una situación en la que se sintiera especialmente relajado, imaginándose por ejemplo que se encuentra estirado en la playa o paseando en el bosque. Debe tomarse el tiempo que necesite para intentar recordar con todo lujo de detalles esa imagen.
- Visualice los colores que le rodeaban, así como los sonidos y los olores. Aumente o disminuya esos sonidos, olores y, en general, las sensaciones.
- Después, intente recordar cómo se sentía en aquel momento, intensificando si lo desea esa sensación de calma y tranquilidad. Puede mover alguna parte de su cuerpo, como por ejemplo las manos para así recordarse a sí mismo esta visualización personal, de forma que siempre que desee realizarla pueda utilizar este gesto o movimiento para traer a la mente su visualización.
- Con la práctica, nada más realizar esa señal, el cerebro encontrará de forma automática el recuerdo de esta situación relajada, sin olvidarse las sensaciones vinculadas a ésta.

Visualización para que desaparezcan las tensiones y preocupaciones

Este ejercicio es muy eficaz si la tensión le impide dormir.

- Como en el ejercicio anterior, adopte una postura que le resulte cómoda, siempre manteniendo los ojos cerrados. Imagínese que sujeta entre las manos unos globos desinflados.
- Después, deje que las preocupaciones aparezcan en su mente. Cada vez que le surja una, imagínese que coge uno de los globos y le pone una etiqueta con el nombre más apropiado.
- A continuación, infle el globo e imagine que lo llena con dicho problema, sin dejar de mirar la etiqueta con el nombre.
- Cuando considere que ya ha liberado todo lo relacionado con ese problema, deje ir el globo y relájese.
- Repita esta operación con todos y cada uno de los problemas que le puedan surgir en la mente.
- Una vez haya terminado, permítase un tiempo para observar y recrearse en la imagen de los globos flotando en el aire. Concéntrese en la sensación de sosiego, mientras realiza varias respiraciones.
- Después, abra los ojos y mueva el cuerpo con lentitud para abandonar la visualización y volver con su actividad normal.

Visualización para crear imágenes positivas

- Al igual que en los ejercicios anteriores, adopte una postura que le resulte cómoda, siempre manteniendo los ojos cerrados. Respire profundamente e imagine que cuenta hasta diez, visualizando cada número en su mente de una forma nítida.
- Tras ver el número diez, imagínese que se encuentra en una habitación (ya sea la habitación en la que realiza los ejercicios de forma habitual, o en otra cualquiera).

- Véase a sí mismo sentado ante un televisor o una pantalla de cine. Intente observar los detalles de dicha habitación para crear una imagen más real.
- A continuación, fije la mirada en la pantalla e imagínese que puede ver ciertas imágenes. Puede recrear imágenes de sí mismo sumido en el estrés, para después verse relajado, o bien recrear una situación del futuro que le preocupa, como por ejemplo una entrevista, una presentación, un examen, etcétera. En este último caso, debe imaginarse que afronta esa situación con mucho éxito.
- Después, deje de mirar la pantalla y vuelva a imaginarse la habitación, dedicando unos minutos a percibir lo relajado que se encuentra, ya sea sentado en un sofá o en otro lugar que haya imaginado.
- Por último, vuelva a visualizar los números en orden inverso, desde diez hasta uno.
- Realice unas respiraciones antes de abrir los ojos y deshacer la postura lentamente.

Bibliografía

Alcaraz, Carmen, *Automasaje para gente muy ocupada. Técnicas de masaje para liberarse en pocos minutos de la tensión y la sobrecarga muscular*, Océano, Barcelona, 2000.

Gurudass, Singh Khalsa, *Kundalini Yoga, tal como lo enseña Yogui Bhajan. Un Yoga teórico-práctico para la nueva era*, Alas, Barcelona, 1983.

Hill, Jacobo, *La salud está en... los métodos de relajación*, Rosaljai, Barcelona, 1996.

Hopkins, Cathy, *101 maneras de relajarse. Cómo evitar el estrés. Una guía práctica para vivir mejor*, Urano, Barcelona, 1998.

Jäger, Gerhard, *La práctica de la relajación. Entrenamiento autógeno*, Everest, León, 1994.

Keers, W.; J. Lewensztain y K. Malavika; *Yoga. Art of Relaxation*, Watkins Publishing, Londres, 1979.

Lam, Kam Chuen, *Tai Chi paso a paso*, Integral, Barcelona.

Monaghan, P. y E. Diereck, *Meditation, the Complete Guide, Novato*, New World Library, California, 1999.

Rosselló, Ramón, *Yoga para gente muy ocupada. Técnicas de Yoga para relajarse y eliminar el estrés en sólo unos minutos*, Océano, Barcelona, 2000.

Sivanda, Sri Swami, *Hatha Yoga*, Kier, Buenos Aires, 1980.

VV. AA., *Técnicas de relajación*. Cuerpomente, Barcelona, 1995.

Watts, Alan, *El camino del Tao*, Kairós, Barcelona, 1976.

Yyengar, B. K. S., *Yoga cien por cien*, Miguel Arimany, Barcelona, 1980.